CAR BUSINESS

YOUR ROAD TO SUCCESS! 101

by: John A. DaRe

This book/guide provides only the Author's / Publisher opinions and neither intends to render legal, accounting or other professional advice with this publication. John DaRe the author, has over 20 years experience in the auto industry, and is trying to share as much knowledge as possible in a book to give guidance into this very lucrative business. You can see more about the Author at: www.CarBusiness101.com

With regards to licensing of a business enterprise or any other legal, accounting or tax matters, the Publisher and Author strongly suggest that the reader seek the services of appropriate licensed professionals and comply with local licensing requirements of the community in which the reader resides or conducts business.

The Publisher and the Author disclaim any personal liability, loss or risk incurred as a consequence of the use and application, either directly or indirectly, of any advice, information, or methods presented in this guide.

ISBN: 1463779488
ISBN-13: 9781463779481

IN THE DRIVER'S SEAT

Wholesale Car Dealer Takes the Road to Success

By Sandy Larson

Home Business Magazine Article / Testimony

Not all car dealers spend their days traversing through maze-like car lots, endlessly negotiating with potential customers. Some car dealers, like John DaRe of Orlando, Florida, actually work from home. "I found out that the typical car lot was not for me," says John, who started buying, fixing up, and then re-selling cars at the age of 16. "Being tied down to one location was too confining."

John entered the auto wholesale industry in 1983 after co-founding Atlantic Auto Brokers Inc. He quickly found this niche to be both personally and financially rewarding. According to John, he and his partner were selling 30-60 cars per month, only working from 9am to 2pm.

Seven years later, John formed his own company, Auto Concepts Inc. Starting out with only himself and one employee; he quickly turned this auto wholesale venture into another success. According to John, he hired eight more people over the next 18 months, and together, they began selling over 2,000 cars a year. "I really didn't know how big of a business this was until then," he recalls. "I was getting more enjoyment out of helping people make money than I was running the business myself!"

After constantly being approached by people who wanted to join his line of work, John eventually put together a book (available at his web site, www.CarBusiness101.com) which shows people step-by-step how to buy cars at or below wholesale and sell them for profit, all from the comfort of their own homes. John also put together a separate program for those who simply wanted to buy cars wholesale, either for themselves or their families.

Today, after 20 years in the industry, John still gets a thrill out of buying and selling cars and enjoys helping others with his auto wholesaling programs. "Our System Locating Vehicles is the main part of the business I concentrate on now—locating cars for people, saving them money, and making a nice profit doing so," he says. "It's a good feeling when everybody wins."

This was a Great Testimony for me coming from a National Business Magazine.

GETTING STARTED IN THE CAR BUSINESS

"Your Road to Success" Starts Here

TABLE OF CONTENTS

CHAPTER I

GETTING STARTED

Once you have made the decision to begin on this road to financial freedom, you must first do a few preliminary items. This chapter will walk you through the basics of Deciding on Your Method for Making Money, Picking A Name, Incorporating or setting up your company, Obtaining a Dealer's License, Obtaining a Bond, and Locating Insurance. Once you complete the simple steps in Getting Started, you will be able to start seeing Profits!

Deciding on Your Method for Profits

Before you take the steps necessary to formulate your business, it is highly recommended that you develop a plan for success. First, read through this entire program. While you are learning how to make this program work for you, remember that you can choose several methods of making Profits. Second, decide on your method. At the outset, you will have two basic options. You can buy cars and retail them to the general public – either through classified ads, word of mouth, auto sales publications or if you are very adventurous through opening a car lot. You can also decide to wholesale vehicles. This would consist of buying cars and re-selling them to other dealers at the auction or at their place of business. Of course, you can make Profits through a combination of both methods but before you begin you should have a strategy for success. This program will show you the basics of purchasing vehicles and then retailing them to the public or wholesaling to other dealers. For more information go to: www.CarBusiness101.com

Name Your Company

Since you will be starting a business to run your car profit system, it is important to establish your new business name immediately. When picking a name for your new company, try to make is simple, a name that is easy to spell. This will save you lots of problems later with titles. Many names with different spellings will cause misspellings at auctions and other dealers that handle your title work. Make sure that you have a few back up names, in case the company name you have chosen has already been taken. You will find out what names are acceptable when you begin Setting Up Your New Company (see below).

It is crucial to choose a respectable name. Your company name is the first thing the public will come into contact with and is sure to make a lasting impression. Do not choose anything like a body shop name or other name that the average person would consider shady or dealing with wrecked vehicles. Remember, if you want to make this your career, take it seriously and be a professional. Image means a lot.

Setting Up Your New Company

Once you have settled on a name (with a few alternate backups) you will need to set up your company. There are several ways to do this and the type of entity you form will depend on your state laws and personal preference. It may be advantageous for you to contact an attorney to file all the paperwork and set up your new company. They should not charge more than $500 for this simple process. If you choose to set up your own entity, most states have very helpful web sites where you can download the proper forms.

Regardless of what form of business you choose to set up, most states will require that you set up a fictitious name to operate under. For instance, if you are going to operate your Car Business under the name "John's Exotic Cars" your state needs to know who is running this business. A fictitious name, also known as doing business as or d/b/a, can be obtained by contacting you Secretary of State and filling out a few simple forms. This registration will also ensure that your name is unique and not being used by another person or company.

Several forms of businesses you can choose to operate include a sole proprietorship, partnership, corporation, or the increasingly popular limited liability company. Sole proprietors and partners do not need to do anything to form their business (with the exception of filing your fictitious name). It is a good idea for partners to have some agreement in writing between the individuals involved, but that is not requires. To actually form a corporate entity – corporation, LLC, etc - states will require that you file paperwork consisting of your company name, company officers, company bylaws, contact information and place of business. This is not a difficult process and most individuals can handle the formation of an entity on their own. It is very important to make sure that you properly notify your state of operation, regardless of the form you have chosen to operate under. This will save you headaches in the future and give you instant creditability with the public.

Below is a very general list of the descriptions of the most popular types of businesses.

- **Sole Proprietorship** – This is a form of business where one person owns all the assets of a business. Besides filing your fictitious name with the state, no formal paperwork is required to begin operating under this business form. As the owner, you will have liability exposure and be responsible for the actions of the business and any debts incurred. Your personal assets could be used to satisfy any judgments, debts or liens incurred by your business. Taxes are paid to the federal government just like you were an individual earning income.

- **Partnership** – One or more people get together and form a partnership. Like the sole proprietorship, no formal documentation (other than the fictious name) is required to begin operating under this business form. Both you and your partners will be jointly and severally liable for the actions of the business and any debts incurred. Your personal assets could be used to satisfy any judgments, debts or liens incurred by a partnership you are involved in – even if you are not a part of the specific transaction. Taxes for each individual are based on the income each partner receives and are paid to the federal government just like you were an individual earning income.

- **Corporation** – A legal entity formed under the authority of the state where you reside. It is separate from the people who own it (shareholders) and provides limited liability for the shareholders. You will need to file documentation, as described by your state, to form a corporation. Most of the time this will include "Articles of Incorporation" and company "Bylaws." These documents are fairly generic, but will have to spell out the purpose of your business and other required information. You, a single person, can form and own a corporation and this entity will protect you from certain liabilities and debt of the company. Normally, you will have to show the public that you are operating as a corporation by adding certain designations (Inc., Co., Corp., etc.) at the end of your company name.

- Once properly formed through your state, your company can choose to be classified as a C Corporation or an S Corporation. The main difference here is how you are taxed at the federal level. An S Corporation has less than seventy-five shareholders and the owners are taxed only once as individuals (sometimes referred to as pass through taxation). A C Corporation is taxed at the corporate level and then the individuals who own it are also taxed. A quick conversation with a lawyer or accountant could help you to make this decision.

- **Limited Liability Company** – This type of entity is also formed pursuant to state law and has attributes of both a corporation and a partnership. You will need to file papers with your state generally referred to as "Articles of Organization." These will be similar to the documents

- Filed by a corporation, but in essence they set out the name, address, members and purpose of your company. A limited liability company is denoted with the letters "LLC" at the end of the name (ex. John's Exotic Cars, LLC). The owners of an LLC are called members and if you (as the owner) are the only member of an LLC, the federal government disregards the entity for federal tax purposes and taxes the income is taxed just like an individual (pass through). If there is more than one member, federal tax treat the entity as a partnership and the federal taxes are assessed on a pass through basis to each member. This entity also provides a liability shelter for the members and the debts and liabilities of the LLC stay with the LLC.

Each state will be different, so be sure to check these entities out before you go forward and ensure that you choose the one that is right for you. You may find that if this is something you are going to do on the side or keep it fairly small in the beginning a sole proprietorship is the way to go. You can always convert into another form if your business grows and dictates the change.

Establishing a Place of Business

In conjunction with Setting Up Your New Company and Obtaining a Dealer's License (see below) it is necessary to establish a place of business for your new company. Most states will not allow you to obtain a motor vehicle license from your home because it is a residential area and your business is seen as a commercial venture. However, a very simple solution to this problem is to rent (or borrow) space from a mechanic, body shop or other business location where you can have a desk and a place to park three to five vehicles outside.

It is normally pretty simple to find someone willing to help you out with this set up and even comes in handy if you buy a vehicle that needs some minor repair work before you resell it. Remember, location is not important if your plan is to wholesale. You should be able to find a place like just to hang your dealer license for about $200 to $300 per month.

If you plan to sell cars from this location, most cities will require you to get an occupational license. This is a fairly inexpensive process and only need to be done if you plan on setting up a car lot. It is a good idea to go through the Car Profit system and figure out how much time and effort you plan on putting into this new venture before you decide to retail cars.

Obtaining a Dealer's License

Once you have selected a name and properly established your new company, you need to obtain a motor vehicle license from the state where you reside. You can either research the requirements for obtaining a motor vehicle dealers license on the Internet or find the closest Department of Motor Vehicle ("DMV") location by looking in the Getting Licensed Volume Two Manual. Each state will have varying requirements, but you should find that you will at a minimum need to fill out an application, include your name, place of business and provide a surety bond (see below). A nominal application fee will probably be required to accompany you application. To show you an example, the state of Florida requires the following items of those seeking to obtain a dealer's license:

Florida General DMV Requirements
- Approval of business location by a DMV representative.
- Completed application form.
- Fee of $300 + - for each main location.
- $25,000 + - surety bond or letter of credit.
- Garage liability insurance.
- Copy of lease for location or proof of ownership.
- Dealer training seminar certificate.
- Registration of fictitious trade name.
- Copy of corporate papers.
- Sales tax number.
- Federal employer identification number.
- Fingerprints and applicable fees.

There are varying types of licenses. The most common types of dealer's licenses are a retail license and wholesale license. Using the state of Florida as an example again, here are the classifications used and some abbreviated descriptions of the types of licenses available as of today.

- **Independent Dealer** — for a person dealing in used motor vehicles only. This license permits the licensee to transact business at retail or wholesale. (This is the type of licenses that the majority will need).

- **Franchise Dealer** — allows the licensee to sell new motor vehicles under an agreement with a manufacturer. This license also permits the licensee to sell used motor vehicles.

- **Wholesale Dealer** — Licensees may only buy from, sell to, and deal at wholesale with other licensed dealers. (The principals learned in the Car Profit system can be utilized with this type of license as well).

- **Auctions** — Are licensed to sell, on behalf of licensed dealers, through the bid process. Auctions may not sell retail.

One helpful thing to keep in mind is that in your application for a motor vehicle dealers license, you may find out it's just as easy to get both a retail license and a wholesale license in one at the same time.

Purchasing a Surety Bond

Most states will require that you purchase a Surety Bond to obtain a dealer's license. A Surety Bond is the way that states ensures car dealers treat the public in a fair and appropriate manner. It is a guarantee of your performance and is primarily in place to ensure the vehicles which you sell to others. It is important to shop around for this bond. There are many companies who specialize in selling Surety Bonds and they are competitive with one another. The dealer Surety Bond should cost around $250 + - per year.

Establishing Dealer's Insurance

In addition to a Surety Bond, most states will require that you secure dealers insurance (also referred to as Garage Insurance) to cover your Liability and the vehicles your purchase and some of the operations of your business. Most dealer insurance policies will cover the cars you purchase as soon as you buy them. These policies are different from your personal auto liability policy, but they are very necessary to protect and you're newfound Car Profits. Again, shop around for insurance! This is a very competitive field and you will find that if you look hard enough you should find good deals. You should be able to get coverage for one - two dealer tags and you as a driver for about $2,000 per year. It is very possible that the same company can sell you a Surety Bond and Dealers Insurance. Remember, you can probably pay your insurance premiums over 6 months if you decide to do so.

Sales Tax Number

Once you establish a corporate entity with the state where you operate, you should also apply for a federal tax identification number and a state sales tax number. The federal ID number will only be necessary if you are incorporated; if you decide to be a sole proprietor you will use your social security number. The state sales tax number in most states will allow you to conduct the transactions of your business (i.e. buying and selling vehicles) without the cost and hassle of paying sales tax on every transaction. Information on the federal ID number can be obtained from the US Department of Revenue. State sales tax numbers will come for your state Department of Revenue.

Miscellaneous Items

Establishing a primary contact number for your new business is very important. This industry relies heavily on contact and sometimes depends on how fast you are able to get in contact with perspective clients. All wholesalers need to be reached within minutes. The most convenient way to establish this contact number is via a cellular phone. Use this number in advertisements, contact information and to conduct your new business. Once this number is established, make sure that you return messages from potential clients in a very timely manner.

Another important way to establish your business and create contacts with potential clients is through business cards. Though it is a very simple step, have business cards made up with your company name and cell phone number. Make sure that the card explains the business you are in and how you can help individuals. Passing out these cards on a consistent basis will begin to spread the word about your newly established business. While at the printers, have them make up your drafts (described in Chapter V).

Dealer Tags

After you have completed all the above items, you are ready to walk into the local Tag Office and apply for your very own Dealer Tags. Most Tag Offices have a Dealer only window; take a copy of your Dealer License, and a copy of your insurance policy along with your sales tax number. In most cases you can walk out with you new tags on the spot. Now how many tags will affect your insurance premiums, so be careful not to get any more than allowed on your insurance.

NOTES: _____

_____

_____

_____

_____

_____

_____

_____

_____

_____

_____

_____

_____

_____

CHAPTER 2

LEARNING THE BASICS

Assuming you have started to set up your Car Business venture, you will need to learn the basics of the car industry. It does not take a rocket scientist to master this business; however a small investment of time and effort to learn about this industry will carry you a very long way. This chapter will walk you through the basics of car industry language, publications, and markets. Some of you will be very in tune to what we are going to discuss and others will be amateurs. Regardless of your expertise, make sure that you read and understand this chapter. It will save you some time and probably some money many times throughout your venture !

Learning the Language

Just as in any industry, car dealers speak a language that is all their own. There are certain buzz words that can clue you into a cars condition, while other less knowledgeable people are left out in the cold. You will find that these words are used at auctions, however most of the time they will be used in conversations with other car dealers at their places of business. It is important to remember that your area will have some buzz words not listed here or some of the definitions below may have a different meaning were you are located. Take caution when first using these words and feel the others out to be sure they know the meaning you are trying to convey!

Let's say you walk onto a car lot, see a car that looks rough, but you know it has potential. You ask the used car manager what he wants for the car and he says "A nickel". Well, don't reach into your pocket and pull out five cents, because he wants $500. So, here are some of the most common terms used in the industry and their corresponding definition.

Nickel $500
Quarter $2,500
Egg beater .... *a car that's a piece of junk*
In the Wrapper ....*A car that is like new*
Hand shaker .... *Standard (manual) transmission*
Knee deep in rubber .... *Tires are like new*
Spiff the car ....*Wash and vacuum*
Detail the car .... *Clean the car, inside and out front and back*
Clock ....*Odometer*
Homerun .... *An exceptionally good profit*
Unit ....*Car*

Learning Your Business

Most people have a basic idea of how much cars are worth on the retail market, but to make serious Car Profits you must know how to buy a car for wholesale prices. One of the best ways to find out about the wholesale pricing for vehicles is through industry publications. Some of the publications will give you detailed information about cars, while other will be a bit more general. Having a publication that lists wholesale prices when you buy a car is crucial. They are quick reference guides that will be your best friend in the industry when used properly. You will very rarely find any serious car dealers who do not have one of these guide handy at all times.

It is highly recommended that you get a subscription to at least one of these publications; otherwise you will be shooting in the dark when attempting to purchase a vehicle. The guides are generally inexpensive, especially considering the benefits you will get by using them. However, if you do not want to make the initial commitment of ordering a subscription, you can purchase some of these pricing guides at some book stores. These guides generally contain a detailed a guide for reading them properly. Make sure you FULLY UNDERSTAND the guide (and the abbreviations contained therein) before you attempt to use them in a vehicle purchase. Not reading them properly could result in paying way too much for a vehicle. Here are some of the most standard car guides and books used in the auto industry:

1. Black Book (updated weekly) / or on your Mobile device
    National Auto Research
    P.O. Box 758
    Gainesville, GA 30503-0758
    1-800-554-1025
    Fax: 1-800-357-3444

2. NADA Book (updated monthly)
    NADA
    8400 West Park Drive
    McLean, VA 22102-9985
    1-800-544-6232
    www.nadaguide.com

3. CPI Book (for specialty cars only, updated quarterly)
    CPI
    P.O. Box 3190
    Laurel, MD 20709
    1-800-972-5312

It is important to note that these books are merely benchmarks and not prices which are set in stone. You will need to take several factors into consideration which only can be determined when looking at the vehicle. These factors include including color, features, and demand for that particular vehicle. While local factors may seem unimportant to be successful you must factor them into your decision on how much to pay for a car. For example, an auto guide may tell you a convertible car you are looking at is worth $10,000 at wholesale. However you know that there is 6 inches of snow outside and no one in your area is going to be strongly considering a convertible at this time of there year. Using some common sense and the auto guides will put you on the road to success in this business.

Another very good method of deciding how much cars are worth is by searching on Cars.com or AutoTrader.com or your local vehicle only classified publication. These types' searches can show you what individuals think their cars are worth. This is a fairly accurate method for determining the retail market, which will in turn help you to decide on a whole sale price.

Finally, reading magazines like "Car & Driver," "Motor Trend," "Auto Week," and other informative magazines will help you learn various car features and trends. It will assist you in knowing the car business and help you to understand the differences between model types, features and options. There could be a $5,000 difference between an EX and a SE model and that is due to the engine type and power accessories. You will need to know this type of information truly make wise transactions.

Learning Your Market

Before you step out to look at cars for this new business you should also take the necessary time to know the markets you will be dealing in. This could be as easy as flipping through the yellow pages or taking a ride around town to scope out the competition. In most areas your landscape will consist of auctions, new vehicle dealerships, used vehicle dealerships and other individual dealers, such as yourself. While this system cannot provide you with local market information, we have listed some of the larger auctions below. You should note that if one of these auction locations is not near you, there should be one located within 80 miles of most major cities and are usually listed in the Yellow Pages. Here are some auction locations and pertinent information:

Mannheim Auto Auctions
P.O. Box 105356
Atlanta, Georgia 30348
(404) 843-5209   www.Manhiem.com

ADT Auto Auctions
3411 Broadway Blvd. S.E.
Albuquerque, NM 87105-0405
(505) 242-9191

Odessa Auto Auctions
11799 New Kings Road
Jacksonville, FL 32219
(904) 768-0029

Angelo-American Auto Auctions
3895 State Road 46 East
Sanford, FL 32771 (407) 323-4090

Another important benefit to being involved with an auction in your area is the market reports that these auction produce. The market reports simply show the vehicles that have run the auction in the past few weeks and give the price that they have sold for. In your Car business, you will find that these guides are extremely valuable and give you the most accurate price for vehicles in your area.

NOTES: _____

_____

_____

_____

_____

_____

_____

_____

_____

_____

_____

_____

_____

_____

_____

_____

CHAPTER 3

APPRAISING A VEHICLE

It has often been said that "**You make money when you Buy**". This principal is very true in the car industry and this should be your motto when trying to maximize your Car Profits. It is crucial that you first buy the vehicle at the right price in order to ensure a profit when you sell it. This chapter will assist you in looking at a car and making an accurate appraisal on the amount you should pay for it.

The Importance of a Buy Figure

The first thing you must do when deciding whether or not to purchase a vehicle is to determine a "buy figure". A buy figure is the amount of money you can pay for the car with the overriding thought in your mind of making a profit on the resale of the vehicle. In order to do this properly, you must appraise the cars value and then work your costs (including profit) into what you determine you can sell the vehicle for.

Before you begin to appraise a car and get that buy figure in your head, you should always know what you are going to do with the vehicle. In other words, where are you going to sell this vehicle and what place will help you to sell it for the most money? As we will discuss in future chapters, there are many places to sell a vehicle – to a private individual, to a dealer or at another auction. If you are aware that a car dealer specializes in a particular type of vehicle or certain makes and models do better at auction, then keep that knowledge at the forefront of your mind when sizing up a vehicle. Knowing your market will help you determine if you can pay a little more for a vehicle. If you are going to retail the car, then you can afford to buy it at a somewhat higher price than if you were going to try and wholesale it to another car dealer.

The better you learn how to appraise a car, the more money you can make. This is a skill that must be developed if you plan on being successful at this venture. One of the easiest ways to learn how to appraise a car's value is to start with the car you currently have. Here is how you would put a buy figure on the vehicle.

Visual Inspection

When you first approach the vehicle, take the intangibles into account. Color, model, features and overall appearance can go a long way once you try to sell this car. A simple question to ask yourself is "Does it currently look good **or** does it have the potential to look good?" Once you have made a general inspection of the cars exterior, open the driver's side door put your head inside the car and check out the interior. Make mental notes of anything you think will need to be repaired or covered up. For instance, there might be a large rip in the front seat, or the dash may be cracked. The carpet could be soiled and the interior dirty – a good detailing could take care of that.

Next, sit down behind the wheel and check how many miles are showing on the clock (odometer). Insert the key into the ignition and start the car. Rev up the engine to listen for any noises that are not natural such as rods or main bearing: Check out: How to inspect a vehicle DVD, more info at www. AutoCheck101.com

Next, sit down behind the wheel and check how many miles are showing on the clock (odometer). Insert the key into the ignition and start the car. Rev up the engine to listen for any noises that are not natural such as rods or main bearing noises. If the engine is quiet and sound, you won't have to allow for any engine repairs. Turn on the air conditioning and make sure it works and blows cold. If it doesn't you will need to make an allowance to have it repaired.

One thing you will want to be aware is not to pass on low mileage vehicles. There is almost always a buyer for a car with low miles. This is just one thing that you can't replace or repair. It is easy to fix a door ding, clean the interior or replace the tires; however miles on a vehicle are probably the single most important factor when appraising a car. Any vehicle with low miles is always worth more than an identical vehicle with higher a mileage reading.

Next, drive the car to make sure the transmission shifts. After you park the car, open the hood. Pull out the oil dipstick and look at it. If the residue on the dipstick is milky white, you have a problem, either a cracked block or blown head gasket. Close the hood and walk around the car. Look for any dents, rust, cracked windows or bad tires.

Calculate the Buy Figure

Now that you know how to properly inspect a car, go do a fair appraisal n the car or cars sitting at your home. It is probably a good idea to take a note pad with you and make some notes about your vehicle. Ask yourself, if I was trying to buy this car to resell and make a profit, how much would I need to buy it for?

Once you have thoroughly inspected the car, then you can begin to figure that buy figure. Pull out your black book or other publication (as discussed in Chapter 2) and look up the car. Write down on a piece of paper what average and rough prices are for the vehicle. If you have registered at an auction, pull out the Auction Reports and look up the vehicle (Auctions & Auction reports are further discussed in Chapter 5). Though you may not find the exact same vehicle in the Auction Reports, try to find a few cars that are comparable, including year, miles, and features. Always look for more than one car in the Auction Reports because you won't now the condition that these cars were in when they sold at the auction. Auction Reports are sometimes better indicators of price than the auto publications, because the Auction Reports give you an accurate representation of the vehicle selling price in your area. Write down the prices that those cars sold for at the Auction.

For example, let's assume that you found your auto pricing publication said that average value is $5,800 and rough value was $5,200. In addition, you found three somewhat similar cars in your Auction Reports. They sold for $5,600, $5,850 and $6,400. The one that sold for $6,400 had 58,000 miles on it and the other two had over 70,000 miles. The car you are looking at purchasing has 66,000 miles, but overall it is in average to good condition. You should immediately decipher that the car you are looking to purchase will probably not sell for $6,400 its miles are significantly higher.

However, by Cost of car...$4,500.00
Transportation back to your shop.......................................50.00
Transportation to Auction..10.00
Detail Car..60.00
Repair Air Conditioner... 180.00
Cost in Car or break-even point 4,800.00

Car sells for..6,000.00
Profit.. $1,200.00

When determining your buy figure, it is best to err on the side of caution than to get yourself into a car for too much money. Always put the figure on any repairs that you need to make on the car. If you don't or you miss something, that's less profit in your pocket.

NOTE: this is an example; you can use this formula for any price range vehicle.

Looking at these auto publications and the Auction Reports, it is safe to assume that this vehicle you are looking at should sell for somewhere between $5,850 and $6,400. To be on the safe side, you decide that if you bought this car it should sell for right around $6,000.

Now that you feel confident that your car is going to sell for $6,000, you must decide how much you should pay for it. One method of determining this buy figure is to back the price down from the amount you can sell it for. The way you do this is simple; you take the costs of getting the car ready for re-sale (covered more in Chapter 7). It is important to include all the costs you will incur, no matter how petty they may seem. You should include items such as transportation, body work, detailing, tires, or repairing the air conditioner. Then decide how much profit you want to make on this car. When determining how much you want to make, be realistic. Your buy figure will ultimately depend on the profit you intend to make and that amount will usually determine if you buy the car or not.

Take all these expenses and add them to your profit. Then take that total number and subtract from the amount you already decided you can sell for car for (in this example $6,000). Now you have your "buy figure".

With all these numbers floating around, it may be helpful to come up with a system or form that you can use for easy calculation. You will find that in the Form Book, we have provided a sample Appraisal Form. Use this form to start out with and then adapt it to the particular needs of your successful Car Profit system. For the sake of discussion we are going to create a sample of a buy figure calculation below.

Selling Price $6,000.00
Transportation back to your shop 50.00
Transportation to Auction 10.00
Detail Car 60.00
Repair Air Conditioner 180.00
Sell fee at auction 100.00
Profit 600.00

What you should pay for car 5,000.00

NOTE: this is an example; you can use this formula for any price range vehicle.

The above example works if you are buying from an auction or an individual, since you can give them a price to begin with. However if you plan on buying any vehicles from other dealers, you may need to adjust your method. If you were at a dealership, the used car manager probably gave you a price somewhere between $5,000 and $5,400 and if it was your lucky day, he may have even said $4,500. Since you still feel the car wills sell for $6,000, you need to back up the price from there.

Again, take all costs (and your profit) into consideration when determining this figure. Let's assume that the used car manager was having a good day and quoted you a price of $4,500. Before you shake their hand and make a deal, add up your costs the other way and make sure that the deal is profitable. Here is how you can do that:

NOTES: _____

_____

_____

_____

_____

_____

_____

_____

_____

_____

_____

_____

_____

_____

_____

_____

_____

CHAPTER 4

FIRST DAY OUT
WHERE TO BUY CARS

Now that you have set your company up and have learned how to properly appraise a vehicle, it is time to put that knowledge to work and start making car profits! As you are probably aware, there are many different places to purchase cars at wholesale prices. You will find as you begin to establish your new car profit business, there are places where you will feel more comfortable in the purchase of vehicles. However at the outset, it is a great idea to try and purchase at least one vehicle from each source listed in this section. Forcing yourself to do this will help you to learn the best places for yourself. This chapter will cover buying cars from New Car Dealers, Used Car Lots, Banks (Repossessed Vehicles), Insurance Companies (Stolen Recoveries), Individuals and Auctions. Let's start at the top.

New Car Dealers

Almost every time a new car is sold off of a lot, the new car dealer takes a used vehicle in on trade. Because the new car dealer is mostly interested in selling new cars, many of the vehicles they take in do not meet their standards for resale at their car lot. It is also possible that thought they like the vehicle their inventory many already be stocked with too many of a particular make and model. That is where you, the wholesaler, come in. New car dealers frequently sell these cars they have taken in on trade to wholesale dealers as an easy and convenient way for them to reduce inventory.

Buying a car at wholesale prices from a new car dealer is much different than just walking around the lot and selecting a car to buy. You will need to find the Used Car Manager and introduce yourself to him/her as an auto wholesaler. There is no magic or secret in being able to buy from that dealer or anyone else. The biggest factor is personality. If the two of you "hit it off", you've won 75% of the battle. At your initial meeting, you will probably be asked what type of cars you buy. Be prepared to give the manager a range of vehicle prices (wholesale of course) that you are willing to buy or explain the types of vehicles you have decided to focus on buying and selling.

For example midsize car up to up to $6,000, compact cars up to $3,500. It is important at the outset to be realistic as most beginning car wholesalers will not be able to walk in and by a $35,000 sports car for resale. If you are not sure what you want to buy from them, then just tell him you buy anything.

Beware, however, that many managers will test you on your first visit.

They will show you some of their old inventory, with the hopes that you'll buy the piece at a high dollar. Don't be afraid to say "No Thanks" on your first visit.

Once you get past any unpleasantries, then move onto business by asking if there are any units they are trying to get rid of and if so, can you take a look at them. Besides trying to sell you a car at a high dollar price on your first visit, the manager will probably show you some other inventory they need to get rid of. In this business your two best options are always: (1) you tell him you can't use that unit at this time, buy you'll keep it in mind or (2) you can make him an offer.

Never hesitate to give a manager an offer lower than what he wants. He is trying to make money for his company, so he'll ask you to pay more than he has in the car. Don't let yourself be intimidated into buying a car. Know your buy figure for the vehicle and stick to it!

Another tactic frequently used at new car dealerships if to package cars and get rid of a few vehicles with one transaction. It is a common practice to put a few rough units and a nice unit together and offer them at a package price. Once you get the package price, sit back and get a "buy figure" on each unit. This will take a little calculation but if you crunch the numbers and figure out that you can make a profit on the package overall then buy it. Honestly it is OK to break even on one vehicle if you feel like you can make $1500 per unit on the other two. Sometimes you have to take these risks to see Car Profits. If you do not feel like the package price is one where you can make money pass on the deal, but make sure you make him an offer first. Make it a reasonable offer, but one you can live with. You will be surprised that a used car manager could take your offer!

Your initial visit should be followed by persistent communication with the dealer. It is a good idea to make a call or stop by at least once per week and checking out what the manager has in inventory. These actions immediately show the manager that you are serious about this business and shows them know you'll be there when cars are available. It is a good idea to do this at several new car dealerships so that you are not stuck into buying inventory for just one location. In all of your transactions with car dealers, you must keep in mind that you are there to make a profit. The manager knows this too, so use it to your advantage and go for purchases at solid wholesale prices!

Used Car Lots

The principles used in buying cars at a new car dealer are basically the same as purchase from a used car lot. These lots take cars in on trade just as the new car dealers do, however you will find that the cars brought in at used car lots are generally much older and not in pristine condition. With those factors in mind, a used car lot is a great place to pick up vehicles at good prices.

Don't overlook the vehicles that look a little rough. There is a market for these vehicles and in this business you will quickly find that a little attention and effort put into the car could yield great dividends. The truth is the used car lot knows that, but they quite often do not have the time, staff or resources to get these cars in to good shape for resale. It is just easier to sell it to a wholesaler and move on to retailing cars to customers.

You should find that these vehicles generally require paint work, tires, detailing or other minor corrections. Keep the costs in mind when determining your "buy figure" and it will be amazing to see the Car Profits you can obtain when you resell a $400 vehicle for $1500 or more. Being patient and making good decisions when buying the units is crucial!

Repossessed Cars

Many times you will find that people try to buy nice cars and for whatever reason are forced into having their cars repossessed. These cars are usually in good shape, however the financial institutions that have taken the cars back have no idea what the cars are actually worth or simply want to get rid of them and focus on other aspects of their business. To find repossessed cars, you need to check with anyone who finances cars such as banks, credit unions, and secondary finance companies. A good place to start is at your local bank and then move on from there. Make a simple inquire and find out who handles repossessed vehicles. Then introduce yourself to that person as a car wholesaler and tell them you are interested in buying vehicles that they repossess. Again, building a relationship at several places is important and will ensure that you have a chance to buy many vehicles at great prices.

Frequently, lending institutions that finance numerous cars may have a holding pen or lot where they send them. If you have established a contact with the business, they will normally allow you to walk the lot and inspect the cars for yourself. Once you have inspected he, you can them make an offer and see what they say. Keep that buy figure in mind and when dealing with a bank you may want to start out low and work up to the figure you actually want to pay. Depending on what the institution has invested in the vehicle, you could find that they are willing to let the vehicle be sold for much less than it is worth.

In addition to having a lot, these financial institutions will employ Recovery Agents to actually repossess the car. Sometimes, these Recovery Agents will also have the responsibility of holding the cars and selling them for the lending institution. When you are talking to the person in charge of the repossessions at the bank, ask them who they use as their Recover Agent. You can also find Recovery Agents in the yellow pages. Either way, get in touch with them and find out if they take bids on any of the cars the repossess. The Recovery Agents may charge a fee for their services, so find out if they charge anything and if so make sure you include their fee when you appraise the car.

Buying repossessed cars can be very profitable for you. If you make the right connections and find repossession sales it could be your own personal gold mine.

Stolen Recoveries

Like financial intuitions, insurance companies find themselves owning vehicles due to their relationships with customers. Many cars are stolen each year and after a certain period of time insurance companies simply pay the owner the value of the car and send them on their way. However, very often you will find that months after the car is stolen and the insurance company has already paid for the car, the vehicle is found. That leaves the insurance company as the owner of a car they do not want. Accordingly, they sell them to the public as a way to recover the money paid out.

Most insurance companies have holding lots at claims offices where they store the vehicles. To locate these lots and facilities where insurance companies store their stolen recoveries, simply look in the yellow pages for insurance claims offices or contact a local insurance agent and ask what their company does with stolen recoveries. Once you have found out where in your area these recovered units are taken, contact the person in charge of that process. As with dealers and banks, forming a working relationship with the person who oversees this program for insurance companies can help you get the most out of this avenue for purchasing vehicles. Sales of stolen recoveries vary from company to company, but you should find that most insurance companies have so many units that they need to sell a few each week. If you are a dealer, you can go to the lots where the cars are sold and inspect them prior to their sale. Take good notes and come up with a solid "buy figure." One important thing to note is that these cars will almost always require some repair work. Remember, they have been stolen and thieves are not too kind to vehicles they do not own. Another thing to keep in mind is that insurance companies sell these cars "As Is." That means regardless of the problems it has, once you buy it you can't return it. Don't let this scare you off, but just be careful to thoroughly inspect the vehicle and take potential problems into account.

The most common way that insurance companies sell their stolen recoveries is through a silent bid. The bids will be due – in a sealed envelope – by a certain date. Once that date arrives, the insurance company representative will open them and the highest bid wins. It does not matter if the highest bid is by $1 or $1000, it wins and you buy the car at that price. You are already prepared to get into a sealed bid because Car Profit has shown you exactly how to establish a "buy figure." That amount is your sealed bid and all you can do after you send it in is hope for the best. Learning insurance sales can take a little time, but finding it and getting the system down can help you to find serious Car Profits!

Individuals

That's right! It is very possible to buy cars at wholesale prices from individuals who are selling cars on their own. Usually they have good reason for doing this and want to get rid of the car quickly so that they can move onto the purchase of something else. The best two places to find out about individuals selling cars is through the classified ads and paying attention to the units parked on the side of the road displaying "For Sale" signs.

Classified ads are a tremendous opportunity for finding cars at great prices and in turn making a lot of money. Many wholesalers have made an extremely good living through the purchase of cars from the newspaper. It is possible that you will find cars advertised below wholesale values. However, don't get discouraged if the prices are all seem too high in the ads. All prices are negotiable and the degree of negotiation will mainly depend on how bad the person wants to sell their car. Find cars listed that you are interested in and then pick up the phone and call them. You may not want to volunteer that fact that you are a car wholesaler, but set up a time to see the vehicle and be prepared to make them an offer. You will find that many people have set the advertisement price much higher than they are willing to take and will drop their price – substantially. Only the seller knows the reason they are selling the car and for how long they have been trying to sell it. Even if you try to by several cars this way and have no success, don't give up. This is a proven method to purchase vehicles at wholesale prices. Before you know it someone will take an offer you have made and then you are on the way to making car profits!

Everyone has been driving down the road and seen the cars with "For Sale" signs all over them. People who puts cars up for sale like this are sometimes more desperate to sell their car or simply do not want to put them in the classified ads. Regardless of their situation, pull off the road and look at the vehicle. Get a preliminary "buy figure" in your head and call the number listed there. The "buy figure" is subject to change based on the interior condition and the engine, however being prepared to buy when the owner comes to show it to you can pay big dividends.

Like vehicles in the classified ads, you may need to attempt to purchase several vehicles like this before you get your first one, but vehicles like this need to be sold otherwise they would not be parked on the side of the road.

You may find that buying cars from individuals is a little more work for you but in the long run gives you better deals. The key here is to be patient and have a solid "buy figure" for each car. Search those ads and watch the roadside on your way to raking in serious car profits!

Auctions

Probably the most intimidating place to buy cars when you are first starting out is the auto auctions. You will be competing against other buyers and wholesalers who are trying to do the same thing you are doing, so beware. We will discuss auctions in much more detail in Chapter 5; however this section will give you an overview of the process of buying units at the auction.

Auctions are a selling place where dealers can meet to sell inventory among each other. These are very fast paced environments and it is crucial that you not get overtaken by the excitement. Being methodical in your dealing at an auction will ensure that you do not pay too much for a vehicle.

At an auction, cars are sold in lanes. There is one auctioneer in each lane and he stands in a location called the box which overlooks the lane. Cars are lined up in the lanes and are then driven, one at a time, in front of the auctioneer. The location where they are bid on is called the auction block, selling block or simply the block. The seller (who normally stands in the box with the auctioneer) tells the auctioneer the specifics of the car and any details he would like the prospective buyer to know, and the auctioneer announces the car.

Before you attempt to buy a car at the auction, you should take some time to simply go there and observe what happens. Pick a lane at the auction and stand there observing what goes on around you. Start with the first lane and work up. Stand close to the auctioneer and watch every car come in. Look at the general condition and miles. Listen closely to the bidding. With each car, make a mental picture of that car and connect it to the selling price. Listen for that magic word, "SOLD," to figure out what really happened while the car was on the block.

Before locking in a price you think the vehicle sold for, watch to see if the buyer goes up to the stand to sign in. These auctioneers are so good you may think he has bids, but he may have never received an actual bid. The auctioneer may run the bidding up himself, hoping to catch a buyer.

This may seem boring after a while, but believe me, this is the best investment of your time. Try to spend at least half an hour in each lane. By changing lanes, you will be exposed to a different selection of vehicles and you will notice a difference in auctioneers.

Once you have experienced the auction, and then try to buy a car there. Select the type of car you want to purchase and then ask the auction office to get you a printout of those types of cars that are selling that day. Next, go out into the staging areas and find the car or cars your want to buy. Inspect each vehicle closely and determine a "buy figure" for the each one. Then you go to the lane (or lanes) where the cars will be running and wait for them to come through. When a car you have selected makes it to the auction block, then you can bid on it. Be sure that you do not go over the "buy figure" you have determined. Cars are sold to the highest bidder, but the seller has the option of accepting or rejecting the highest bid. If you are the highest bidder and the seller agrees to sell the car, then you have bought it.

It is important to note that you will make money on these cars only if you purchase them at the right price. This section has provided you with a very basic introduction to buying cars at the auction. Chapter 5 will take you much more in depth and provide you with the insight you need to make Car Profits at any auto auction.

As we have shown you, vehicles can be purchased almost anywhere. Regardless of where you buy your vehicles from, make sure that you go through all the steps covered in Chapter 3. No matter who is selling you the car, your Car Profits will only show up if you properly appraise the vehicle and purchase it at a "buy figure" where you can make money!

NOTES: _____

_____

_____

_____

_____

_____

_____

_____

_____

_____

_____

_____

_____

_____

_____

_____

_____

_____

CHAPTER 5

LEARNING THE MARKET GOING
TO AUCTIONS

Chapter 4 gave you a brief introduction to car auctions, however as you will quickly find these avenues for buying and selling vehicles can be complicated at times. This chapter will walk you through the basics of auto auctions and also show you how profits can be made through buying and selling vehicles at various auctions. Many car dealers have determined that buying cars at wholesale prices and then reselling them in the wholesale market is a great way to make a living. Of course, you will have to decide for yourself and this chapter is just the place to start.

Most auctions are for registered auto dealers only. Volume 4, Making Contacts will give you a list of some auctions that may be located near you. This is by no means a comprehensive list; however it should provide you with a starting point. If you live near a major metropolitan area, pick up your phone book and see if there are any local auctions listed in the Yellow Pages. Once you have selected an auction or auctions that are nearest to you, make a trip to those locations and get signed up to be a member. The fees are reasonable and being a member of at least one auction gives you the access to a valuable market for doing business.

We have previously noted that auto auctions are your best way to learn the market! This exercise, described in Chapter 4, cannot be stressed enough. To fully realize car profits you must invest some time and preparation into this new venture. Be sure that once you are registered at an auction you take the time to go there and simply observe the dealings that take place.

Scope Out Your Vehicle(s)

Prior to jumping right up to the auction block and bidding on cars, you must determine which cars you want to bid on. The only way to do this is by inspecting the vehicles while they are parked in their staging positions or in line to be auctioned. Most dealers have found that it is very helpful to have an idea of the type of vehicle you need to buy before going to the auction location. We would suggest getting to the auction at least one hour before it is scheduled to begin. Upon arrival, go to the auction's help counter and request an inventory list for that day. Because the complete vehicle list at most auctions will be very lengthy (up to 6,000 vehicles in one day), you will need to be specific and request specific vehicle models and years. Let's assume that in your first trip to the auction you have decided to look at 2004 – 2009 Nissan Altima's. While auction reports will vary based on the auction preferences, you should receive a printout that looks something like this:

Lane	Run	Year	Make	Model	Sub series	Color	Doors	Cyl	Trans	Int	Miles
14	75	2008	Nissan	Altima	GXE	GRAY	4	6	Auto	L	39,576
14	76	2009	Nissan	Altima	GLE	RED	4	6	5	C	16,032
14	77	2008	Nissan	Altima	GLE	MAR	4	6	5	C	44,976
14	104	2004	Nissan	Altima	GLE	BLK	4	6	Auto	C	72,543
16	12	2005	Nissan	Altima	SE	GRN	4	6	Auto	C	69,398
8	99	2004	Nissan	Altima	SE LIM	SILVER	4	6	Auto	L	55,487
8	103	2006	Nissan	Altima	GXE	SILVER	4	6	Auto	L	36,103

From this printout, you can devise a plan to inspect the cars you are interested in and be ready for them when they come up to the auction block. You will see from this example that it is sometimes difficult, if not impossible, to bid on every car yourself because they can run at the same time in different lanes. Getting this list will help to you to focus on the cars you want to select and assist you in determining which cars will lead you to car profits.

Continuing with our example, let's assume that you have decided to focus on 4 of the cars listed. Our choice was based on mileage, demand and our availability to thoroughly inspect these cars before they make it to the auction block. We recommend that you use this list obtained from the auction as a working list, just in case you want to see eliminated cars later.

Setting Your Buy Figure

Prior to the vehicles being run through the auction block, they are parked in a staging area around the auction. Most auctions allow you to go to the cars and perform an inspection, as long as you do not move the car out of line. The inspection you will perform is exactly the same as we practiced in Chapter 2 – Appraising a Vehicle. This is you opportunity to determine your Buy Figure and get ready for the fast paced action that occurs when the car is on the auction block. It is very helpful to take you working vehicle list and make notes about the cars beside their information.

It is crucial for you to stay current with auction prices. Market values change of vehicles change for a variety of reasons, but the values tend to fluctuate on a regular basis. Different times of the year the market is stronger. The very obvious example of this cycle is apparent in convertibles. There is a high demand (higher prices) for these cars in the summer and a lower demand (lower prices – right time to buy) in the winter. If you stay on top of the changes in pricing, you will quickly find that you industry knowledge will bring serious Car Profits. The easiest way to stay informed is to read the weekly auction reports, which lists each car sold, miles, features and price. After a few weeks, you will start to see the trends and values for particular makes and models that interest you. These reports come in very handy when standing next to a vehicle and determining a Buy Figure.

When buying a car, first look at it and decide "Where am I going to sell it – what auction – what other dealer?" Then buy according to what you can get back at the auction or where ever you decide to sell the car.

While at these vehicles, take a moment to check previous auction reports (that you have brought with you) and the used car pricing guides. Make sure you also determine where you are going to try and sell the car. If you want to re-sell at another auction, then make sure you calculate for a lower selling price, however if you are going to try to retail the car you can give yourself some room to move, based on your anticipated selling price. At this point, it is necessary to settle on a Buy Figure. Write this number down on your working list and stick to that number when bidding on the car – this takes out the guess work and nervousness when bidding on a car.

Lanes

Once you have inspected all the vehicles you are interested in, it is now time to formulate a plan and head over to the auction lanes. From our list, we can see that 3 of our cars run in succession early in lane #14. The other car we like runs at a later number in lane #8.

Now that we have chosen and inspected our potential vehicles, the auction lanes are our next stop. As we have discussed, cars being sold at auction run in lanes. At the auction, above the auctioneer, there are colored lights. Each time a new car comes up to the auction block, the lights will change color to indicate the condition of the vehicle or other specifics as listed below. These lights are very important and can have a definite impact on the value of the car. Some of the most common lights you will see are:

Red light .... usually as is
Yellow light .... caution announcement
Green ....ride and drive
Blue ....no title present
White .... Over 100,000 miles

Every auction has their own rules and you should learn the general rules for each auction. Since you are familiar with how the auction works (Chapter 4), you know that when your cars come to the block they will be there for 30 to 60 seconds at the most. Having your working list with the Buy Figures for each car very accessible is important. At most auctions a simple flip of the hand, nod of the head or sudden movement will get the auctioneers attention. To bid you simply acknowledge you willingness to pay the price which is being announced? If you are the high bidder and the seller accepts the price, you have bought yourself a vehicle at the auction. Chapter 6 will walk you through the basics steps of a Transaction at the auction.

Secrets of the Auction

Many auctions are big; they have four to twelve lanes of cars running at the same time. Should you stumble into a lane where there are little to no bidders standing around the lane and the dealer who has a car on the block needs for that car to go away, you will have a great chance to make a quick buy. These situations happen every once in a while, but you should make sure that you are confident doing a quick appraisal and calculating a Buy Figure in your head on the sport. Having your auction reports and a used car guide is helpful in making a quick decision. Looking over the last few weeks of the auction reports is the best, and safest, way to determine what profit you could make on a vehicle. Remember, the Black Book and NADA Book are only guides. Auction reports show you exactly what the vehicle is bringing in your area…buy according to them. The key in this situation is once you get set on a Buy Figure; send in a bid that is much lower than you want to pay. You can always increase your bid, but the auction never allows anyone to back off their bid when you are the highest bidder.

They way you make money buying cars at auctions is knowing what cars bring the most money at which auctions. Auctions have personalities and once in the business, you will quickly learn the reputations and types of cars that do well at the various auctions. For example: You've been studying cars at ABC Auction and you see that midsize GM cars with under 100,000 miles on them bring a lot of money at this auction but high mileage (over 100,000 miles) imports do extremely poor. You realize immediately that the cars at XYZ auction are just the opposite. High mileage imports do well there while mid-size GM cars don't. So now you start looking to buy mid-size GM cars at XYZ auction and you sell them at ABC auction. And at ABC auction you watch and buy high mileage imports and sell them at the XYZ auction. Some auctions do well with clean late model cars. If some older high-mileage car comes through, you won't have many bidders on it. You may be able to purchase it at a bargain price and run it to an auction that sells mostly that type of car. It is very important to learn what cars sell well at each auction. You may get good enough that all you need to do is work several auctions a week to make a decent living.

One other thing you should be aware of is to be sure you look around and see who you're bidding against. Some wholesalers and dealers may have planted certain people to "bid up" their cars to a certain dollar figure. At that time, you make the decision whether you want the car or not. Remember, the person selling the car doesn't have to sell unless he wants to, so make sure you pick more than one or two cars to bid on.

NOTES: _____

_____

_____

_____

_____

_____

_____

_____

_____

_____

_____

_____

_____

_____

_____

_____

_____

CHAPTER 6

PREPARING A VEHICLE FOR RESALE

Now that you have purchased a vehicle, the next question should be … what should I do to get this thing sold and receive my Profits? As we discussed in Chapter 3, the better Appraisal you do on a vehicle the more prepared you will be to turn that car into serious Car Profits. It is always best to buy cars that do not need much work, because that is less work for you and less money you have to put into each vehicle. However, many dealers have made a handsome living taking a car no one else wants and doing a few minor things to put it in tip top shape. Proper reconditioning of your vehicle can be the difference between a profit or a loss. It may also be the deciding factor on whether you make a profit or a homerun when you sell the car.

The major items you should be aware of are as follows:

1. Body
2. Paint
3. Interior
4. Engine & Transmission
5. Tires
6. Air Conditioning & Windows
7. Detail

This chapter will take you through the basics of how to properly recondition a vehicle and prepare it for sale! Before we get started, it is very important to note that you success in this business will depend in part on your ability to develop good working relationships with businesses that specialize in the above listed areas. A good body shop or air conditioner repair man can save you hundreds of dollars and make sure that your vehicle always look and run great. Check out www.AutoCheck101.com for more detailed info on inspecting a vehicle...

Body

Most dealers prefer to buy a car that is ready to put on their front line with little to no work. The larger dealers will not even bother buying a car with damage and this is your opportunity to get a vehicle at a good price. Obviously any dealer can demand more money for a car that is in pristine shape than for a car that has a major dent or two in one of the panels. Spotting potential goldmines with minor damage can be very profitable, but you must become very familiar with what it costs to fix damaged items. If you spot a car with several door dings, then you better buy it cheap enough to repair or sell it as is and still make a profit. It is crucial that you develop a working relationship with at least two body shops. One that you can send your late model cars to when you need the body and paint work to look flawless, and another body shop where you can send your older cars and get a complete paint job at a reasonable price. Before you buy any really damaged or wrecked cars, make sure your body shop can do collision work at reasonable prices. If not, find a competent body shop that can.

Paint

When it comes to painting the car, never change the color. It takes away from the value. If it is a late model car that a new car store would want, the paint needs to when it comes to painting

the car, never change the color. It takes away from the value. If it is a late model car that a new car store would want, the paint needs to be almost perfect. If it's an older car, you don't have to be so picky, but the shinier the car, the better it looks, and the more money you can sell it for. A little word of caution: be careful about buying a car in the rain. No matter how bad the paint job is, the car will still look good.

On an older car, you can usually get a reasonable price for an overall paint job from one of the many franchise paint shops. Take a little time and visit them, and ask to see some of their finished products before you give them any work. You will be able to tell who you want to use to work on your cars on the future. Check out www.AutoCheck101.com for more details…

Interior

Again, you need to check around and find someone that can do good interior work at a reasonable price. You will need someone that can repair leather, vinyl, or cloth interiors. Generally, you will not have to worry about headliners. Even though they will improve the look of the vehicle, they will not increase the value.

It's important to have relationship with someone who is knowledgeable and does excellent work on vehicle interiors. It is not uncommon to run across a 3 to 5 year old car with leather interior that is all cracked and torn, but has an extremely low price. Just like body work, most dealers do not want to deal with these issues. Even your first impression of the car may be one of disgust, however with a little time and effort you can make the seats look like new and make yourself a nice car profit.

One word of caution that you be aware of is that dashboards are usually a very expensive item to be replaced. They generally always have to be replaced, as repairing them is not too feasible. Their replacement is extremely labor intensive and could end up costing you significant money. If you spot a vehicle with dash board cracks or other issues, buy it accordingly. Most dealers will not go to the time or expense of replacing these items, but have found that molded dash covers are sometimes and acceptable alternative. Shop around for good prices, but beware when looking a car with dashboard cracks.

Carpet is another item that is very cumbersome and expensive to replace. Look at the carpet in each vehicle carefully before you buy, however if you get a deal that is too good to pass us you have several options. Replacement is an expensive process, but may be worth it in higher end cars. A nice set of floor mats will improve the look of a vehicle with damaged carpet, but again, not the value. Make sure that you also look at the carpet in the trunk. This is where most spills happen and can sometimes be overlooked during the excitement of an auction.

Engine & Transmission

When you purchase the car, make sure the engine doesn't have any knocks or strange sounds. It does not take a rocket scientist or a trained mechanic to be able to tell when an engine has had its better days. Experience has shown that these cars are generally the ones you want to stay away from. There is nothing worse than buying a car with what you think is a simple engine problem and then taking it home to find out you need extensive work done to it in order to have it prepared for sale. One method of attempting to find problems in an engine is to rev that engine up while in idle. Roll the window down during your initial inspection and listen for anything out of the ordinary. If you want to take a chance on buying a car with what appears to be engine problems, buy the car cheap enough so you can have it repaired.

Another important aspect of the mechanical make up to the vehicle is the transmission. If you have the opportunity to drive or ride in the car before you buy it, be sure to take advantage of that opportunity. If you feel a hard shift or the car hesitates before its shifts between gears you may have a transition problem. Again buy cautiously in these situations and leave yourself enough room to sell cheap or get it repaired.

What you are planning to do with the vehicle can help determine what you do about a transmission problem you discover. If you're going to place the car with a customer or attempt to sell it into the retail market, you'll want to make sure it shifts okay. This could require getting your transmission repairman to make the necessary adjustments. However if you're going to sell it at an auction, you can usually leave it the way it is. If you choose this route, be prepared to take less for the car. You may still make money on it without having it repaired. Check out www.CarBusiness101.com for more details...

Tires

Tires can be a tricky issue. When you buy a car, be sure to check out what kind of condition the tires are in, but always remember that these are the easiest parts to replace. You can generally get a good set of tires for less than $400 +. While tires may not sell the car for you, they can help to influence a customer's decision. If you have a late model car that you care going to sell to a new car dealer, then make sure it has good and matching tires. For any other customer it is sometimes best to leave the tires the way they are unless they are in such bad condition that they make the car look bad. .

Air Conditioning & Windows

Depending on where you live, AC can be a very important factor in how much money you get for your cars. If you live in a warm climate and it is not winter, then you should make sure the air conditioner blows cold. Conversely, make sure the heat works in cooler climate areas. As with other items around the car, you should find a good Heating and AC that is up to date on all the systems. Shop around some and find someone who will give you a reasonable price and ensure that your work is always handled properly.

The first thing a potential driver will see when they test drive your car will be through the car windows. Make sure that the windows are cleaned and that they are not missing or broken.

Missing windows and windows with significant damage should be replaced. Cracked windows or electric windows that don't work are not too big of a problem. Try to sell the car the way it is. Some customers may demand a discount for those problems, but those discounts usually cost less than the actual work.

Detail

Make a conscious effort to always present your cars in good condition. That means the following should all be cleaned: engine, trunk, door jambs, interior, tires and wheels. Have the paint buffed and waxed. Find a person who will detail your cars and who will pay attention to the little things. It is not uncommon for car dealers to find a good worker and actually hire them to clean their cars full time. The value of a good detail is very high. There are quite a few detailers out there but not many of them do the kind of work you would expect. Stay on top of their work and make them redo anything that is not right. Make sure that your cars are clean, neat and ready to shine. The first impression of a car is always crucial and may be the deciding factor for your customer.

The best advice we can give you when preparing a car for resale is to no get caught up in fixing items which will not make you money. There is no need to fix minor items as they will generally cost more to fix than the increase in the cars value. Make sure the care is clean and presentable when showing to customers. If your customers are too picky, you can politely remind than that they are buying a used vehicle and there will be some items that are not going to be perfect. Having your cars prepared properly for resale is an important aspect if this business than many people overlook. Take the time and effort to pay attention to this area and you should find yourself making Car Profits! Check out www.CarBusiness101.com for more details… for your Business Plan!

NOTES: _____

_____

_____

_____

_____

_____

_____

_____

_____

_____

_____

_____

_____

_____

_____

_____

CHAPTER 7

MAKING Car Profits... SELLING THE VEHICLE

Now that you have bought the vehicle and prepared it for sale, the only thing left to do is sell that car and realize you're Car Profits. Selling cars is much easier than you may think and you do not have to turn into that pushy sales person you dread to see coming out of the car lot doors to be successful at it. All it takes is some knowledge, a little persistence and a positive attitude. There are various methods and avenues for selling cars and this chapter will walk you through the three most popular: Auction, Other Dealers, and Retail.

Actions

At this point in the manual, you probably know that the most obvious place to sell cars is right back at the Auction. When the market is hot, this is the best and most cost efficient way to sell your cars. For example, you purchased a vehicle that you thought would make $800, you take it to the auction and it makes you $1,200. That's an additional $400 you would have left on the table or you would have sold the car to another dealer. As discussed in Chapter 5, it is possible to make car profits by simply buying the right car at one auction and taking it to another auction for re-sale. This method can be used very successfully, but you must know your market and be aware of the price fluctuations at the different auction sights.

When you first get on the block with the auctioneer, he will ask you if you have the title to the car. If you have not have the title to the car, for whatever reason, he will turn on the blue light and the auction will charge you a title fee. The auctioneer will probably ask if the miles are over or under 100,000. If they are over, he will turn on the white light. You also need to tell the auctioneer anything about the car you want the potential buyers to know. For instance, if the car has a diesel engine, no air conditioning, weak clutch or worn C.V. joints. For any of these announcements, the auctioneer will turn on the yellow light. However, remember that another advantage of selling cars at an auction is that you are under no obligation to tell the buyer any history of the car. It is up to them to research if the car has any mechanical problems. You should not only tell him weak points to the car, but be sure to highlight the positives you see in the vehicle. This may help the vehicle sell and bring other dealers to become interested in your vehicle.

Now the fun begins. You sit back and watch others bid on you vehicle. Make sure you tell the auctioneer what you want to get for the vehicles. He will then work towards getting that price. Remember the auction staff generally works on commission and they will do everything possible to make sure a sale happens. When the buyers get to a price you will accept, the car is sold. It sometimes takes a few weeks for a car to sell, but in time you will turn your investment into Car Profits.

Other Dealers
Taking quality used cars to a car lot is something that can be beneficial to both you and the dealer. You will have your car sold and the will get a vehicle that is good shape without having to search too hard. It would be to your advantage to develop a relationship with several new car stores and small independent

used car lots. On numerous occasions, when you're looking at a car to purchase, you can call the lots you think may be interested in purchasing the car for the price you'd like to ask. Describe the car to them and have them give you a "buy figures" over the phone. Now you have the car sold before you even bought it! By doing this, you can build in the auction sale fees, transportation and detail costs into your bid and make sure that you come out of the deal with car profits. These costs can quickly add up to several hundred dollars and by figuring those into the bid you make you will ensure that you come out with a deal worth while. The longer you are in this business the more knowledgeable you will become about dealers in town. If you know that ABC dealer likes high end import cars, then when you see one up for sale it is quite possible that they will buy this from you. One important point to remember is never try to push a bad car on someone that buys from you on a regular basis. You may destroy your relationship with a good buyer which would cripple your business – and your profits.

Retail

Finally, you can retail the car. Many dealers specialize in finding cars which are popular with the public and selling them directly into the retail market. It is most common to advertise these cars for sale in your local newspaper or Auto Trader publication. Besides finding a car that the public tends to like, there are some other reasons to do this. First, you may have paid too much for the car, in which case you would lose your profit, maybe some of the investment, if you wholesaled it. Perhaps the engine blew up or the transmission went out. You're looking at a $500 loss if you sold it wholesale. Simply advertise the car and retail it for a profit.

Retailing a car is something you may always want to keep in mind. This is a little harder than working with dealers, because you actually have to sell the car to a consumer. However, this is generally your most profitable method to make Profits. This avenue of sale may take a bit longer than selling via auction or to another dealer, but in the end the increased profits can be worth the wait. You may want to keep one car in the paper all the time for retail so you can make a $2,500 to $3,000 profit. Only one a month would certainly add to the bottom line. Check out www.CarBusiness101.com for more details...for a Perfect Business Plan... !

Regardless of how you decide to sell the vehicles you buy make sure that you always deal with your buyers truthfully and respectfully. Many dealers and consumers will work with you time and time again, if you simply treat them fairly and sell them a reputable vehicle.

NOTES: _____

_____

_____

_____

_____

_____

_____

_____

_____

_____

_____

_____

_____

_____

_____

_____

_____

_____

CHAPTER 8

IMPORTANT TIPS FOR MAXMIZING Car Profits

Now that you have made it to the last chapter of Volume 1, you are well on your way to making Car Profits. There are just a few other things that you should learn about before you embark on this new venture. While the regulations on titles, forms and other aspects of the car business may vary from state to state the following information should give you a basic understanding of what you need to look out for, you may also want to check out: www.CarBusiness101.com

Surprisingly, there is very little in the way of required forms when it comes to purchasing cars, other than what the company or auction you purchase cars from may require for their own personal files. Be sure to check with your state Department of Motor Vehicles to ensure that you are properly filling out all the necessary paperwork. You can use Volume 2 to find your state DMV.

Wholesale Order
A wholesale order is a very common form that dealers use to purchase a car. It is a contract for sale, but since vehicle transactions are very common this form simplifies the process. Take some time to review the Wholesale Forms and read the fine print. The form is very easy to fill out and basically requires minimal information about the vehicle. The seller is normally the one who fills this form out. As with many of the forms, the necessary

paperwork can be purchased from a clearing house such as Gallaher Promotional Products or can be printed through you local print shop. At a minimum, your Wholesale Order Forms should contain some legal language evidencing an agreement between the seller and buyer. It should also include most, if not all, spaces for the following items:

1) Seller's name, address and phone number.
2) Your company name, address and phone number.
3) How the vehicle is being paid for (cash, check, and draft)
4) The Price (in words AND numbers)
5) Exact mileage on the odometer, including any special designations for cars with over 100,000 miles. .
6) Vehicle makes (Chevrolet, Ford, Chrysler, etc.).
7) Vehicle model (Corvette, Mustang, etc.).
8) 2 door or 4 doors.
9) Vehicle Identification Number ("VIN"). It is a seventeen (17) digit number and will be located on the front left side of the dashboard or inside the driver's side door. It is also a good idea to check the year of the car again. You would do this by looking at the VIN and count over to the 10th digit. This digit tells you the year of the car. In your black and gray book just after the reference, there is a table telling you what each digit stands for. For example, if the 10th digit were an L, the year would be 1990.
10) Year Vehicle was produced.
11) Seller's signature (this is the only part that the seller does.)
12) Current date.
13) List your company address.
14) Your signature.

Wholesale Orders should be carbon copies and after it is completed and signed, the seller keeps the top copy and you keep the bottom one. Upon completion of the form the car is legally the purchasers and you should work out the payment as specified on the order. Money between dealers is generally not exchanged until a clear title is presented by the seller.

Titles

Titles are very important. Titles are money. This is the document generally issued by the state DMV which identifies specific vehicles and who owns them. If the numbers on the title do not match up identical to the VIN numbers on the car, then you do not own that car. This is an area most beginning dealers tend to overlook, however it is one area that you should take your time on. When you pick up a title, it is very important to double check all information. Check the Draft (discussed below) or Wholesale Order that you used to buy the vehicle, all identification numbers must match perfectly, check mileage on top of title and bottom of title to make sure the match your draft and that you took all numbers off the vehicle correctly.

If any discrepancy is found on any of the numbers, do not pick up the title. The selling dealer is responsible to make any and all corrections needed to give you a clean title. They have title clerks on their payroll to handle this. When you are a selling dealer, it is important that you or someone you trust handles this process for you. We would recommend that you find very competent title agencies to assist you with this process. When you first begin, they will be an unbelievable resource and can guide you through this potential minefield. Most independent dealers have used the same title agent for years. It is much more profitable for you to be selling and buying cars than dealing with the paperwork that accompanies title transfers and changes.

Most titles can be assigned from dealer to dealer by filling out the back of the title issued by the state. Sometimes, if a vehicle has been moved from dealer to dealer a few times, you may need to use a title reassignment form. This form is filled out by the seller if there is no room on the title to reassign the car to you. When you buy the car, the dealer will give you your copy. When you sell the car, you have to fill out one of these forms to go with the title, including the title reassignment form you received from the original seller.

If you sell a vehicle to a consumer, you will need to file the appropriate paperwork with the state and any lending institution involved in financing the vehicle for the buyer. This is an area where having a title agency to perform this work, can help your business tremendously. You can figure the cost of transferring the title and tag into the price of the car and then hand off this paper heavy task to a person who specializes in dealing with the DMV.

Drafts ... Buying With No Money

This business is one of the few that you can actually buy cars, trucks, boats, trailers, etc. with no money. It's accepted thousands of times ever day in place of a check and it's called a draft. The main reason drafts are used in this business is because there is a lag time in getting vehicle titles from one buyer to another seller. Normally, drafts are not accepted at auctions. You will find that the most common place to use drafts is in a dealer to dealer transaction.

The most frequently used type of draft is an envelope draft. It is nothing more than an envelope with all the information on filled in on the outside of it – buyer, seller, and type of vehicle. Most print shops know exactly what this is used for and can help you select the right draft for your business. You can also choose to put your logo or other identifying mark on the draft to distinguish it from others.

Drafts are used just like a check. A draft is a legally binding document that represents a good faith offer which basically says, the issuer of the draft (you) has agreed to pay X amount of dollars for a specific vehicle, make, model, ID#, and miles. Once you have filed out an envelope draft, you should remove your copy from inside the envelope and give the envelope to the seller. When the seller accepts the draft, they have agreed to that price and a contract between you two has been established. The evidence of the contract is the draft you have exchanged.

At the time you give the draft to the seller, you can take the vehicle with you and in essence have purchased the vehicle. The seller will do the title work and will contact you when the title to the vehicle is ready. Once the title is ready for delivery, then you should carefully review the title for any errors (as described above), and pay the seller with a real company check. You will then have a good sellable title to the vehicle.

Make sure that once you pay for the car and you receive the title to the vehicle you purchased, you pick up the draft from the seller.

Drafts can take on many different forms, but at a minimum, they should include the following items:

1) Name of the company you are purchasing the vehicle from.
2) Amount you are paying.
3) Write in amount you're paying.
4) Enter the current date.
5) Stock number of car if dealer has one.
6) Year vehicle.
7) Make and model of vehicle.
8) Vehicle identification number.

9) Number of cylinders of engine (4, 6, or 8).
10) Color of vehicle.
11) Odometer reading.
12) Odometer reading.
13) Seller signs his name.
14) Date filled out.
15) Your signature.

What a draft does for you is simple. It enables you to have the vehicle in your possession, with no money out of your pocket, to sell for a profit. You are now prepared to sell the car to a dealer or at an auction. Make sure you are somewhat cautious when you start using drafts. You do not want to end up in a situation where you have purchased several vehicles via the draft method and then when the time come to actually present a check you have no funds to actually pay the seller. Drafts can be a great tool in the business, but be sure you do not get carried away.

A typical situation for using a draft goes something like this. You buy a car with a draft from Dealer A. You then take the car to Dealer B and he wants to purchase that car. The new owner (Dealer B) will give you a draft because, as of yet, you have not title. When Dealer A calls you and says he has the title for your vehicle, you then call Dealer B and tell him you have the title. Also mention that you would like to stop by "in the morning" to drop off the title and pick up a check. Then, the next morning, stop by Dealer A with your company check and pickup your title. Then go to Dealer B, drop off the title and pick up your check (with your profits). You just made $500-$1,000 on a car with no money out-of-pocket!

A real life example of this situation can also be used at the auction. Because you are aware to the market you know that Honda Accords sell very well at your local auction.

You happen to be at a dealership who wants to get rid of an Accord and you recognize that this could be resold at the auction for a good price. Once you agree upon a price you will write the dealer a draft for the price and take the car to the auction. You will sell the car at the auction with no title. Most auctions require that you provide the title to the purchaser within 30 days of the sale. Once the car is sold at the auction, your title from the original dealer should be ready. Again, you go to the dealer, get the title and drop off a check. Then you provide the title to the auction and receive your money for the sale of the Accord.

In both these instances you were able to move cars and make a profit without ever coming out of pocket to actually by the cars. As we stated earlier, if it takes you a while to sell a car that you have purchased with a draft you should be prepared to buy it. Drafts are a form of contract and you must be prepared to provide real money to the seller when they are able to furnish you with a good title.

One very important thought. NEVER give anyone a check for a car if a good sellable title is not present. A draft also serves as a form of protection for both parties.

Conclusion

Congratulations!!!!! You have now reached the end of Volume 1. Make sure to study the other Volumes included in the Car Business guide to assist you in your new venture. Experience has proved that if you follow the principles set forth in this book, work hard and be persistent you can make serious Car Profits. Don't be discouraged if it takes you a few weeks or even months to learn the business. This book is a result of over 20 years of experiencing the ups and downs in the car business. It has given you a great advantage to go out there and make Car Profits;

however you should make a conscious effort to learn the business by getting out there and seeing how it works for yourself.

If you need some additional information with a Car Dealer Business Plan, check out:

www.CarBusiness101.com for more details…

We wish you much success in your new business and look forward to hearing the success stories as you get out there and make Car Profits!

NOTES: _____

_____

_____

_____

_____

_____

_____

_____

_____

_____

_____

_____

_____

_____

_____

"Getting Licensed"

Becoming a Dealer.
Your First Step!

Contact Information
On Your Local "DMV."
Department of Motor
Vehicle Office

Listed Alphabetically By State -
Also Agencies and Other Organizations

DEPARTMENT OF MOTOR VEHICLE ADDRESSES

ALABAMA DEPARTMENT OF PUBLIC SAFETY
500 Dexter Avenue, Montgomery AL 36104
Phone: 334-242-4400

ALASKA DEPARTMENT OF MOTOR VEHICLES
2150 E. Dowling Road, Anchorage, AK 99507
Phone: 907-269-5551

ARIZONA DEPARTMENT OF TRANSPORTATION
P.O. Box 2100, Mail Drop 500M, Phoenix, AZ 85001-2100
Phone: 602-255-8152

ARKANSAS OFFICE OF DRIVER SERVICES
7th & Wolfe Street, Joel Ledbedder Building, Room 126
Little Rock, AR 72203
Phone: 501-682-7060

CALIFORNIA DEPARTMENT OF MOTOR VEHICLES
2415 First Avenue, Sacramento, CA 95818
Phone: 916-657-7677

COLORADO DEPARTMENT OF REVENUE
MOTOR VEHICLE DIVISION
1881 Pierce Street, Lakewood, CO 80214
Phone: 303-205-5600

CONNECTICUT DEPARTMENT OF MOTOR VEHICLES
60 State Street, Wethersfield, CT 06161
Phone: 860-566-4710

DELAWARE DEPARTMENT OF PUBLIC SAFETY
MOTOR VEHICLE DIVISION
P.O. Box 698, Dover, DE 19903
Phone: 302-739-2500

DISTRICT OF COLUMBIA
BUREAU OF MOTOR VEHICLE SERVICES
301 "C" Street, NW, Washington, DC 20001-2100
Phone: 202-727-1159

FLORIDA DEPARTMENT OF MOTOR VEHICLES
2900 Apalache Pkwy, Room B435, Neil Kirkman Building,
Tallahassee, FL 32399
Phone: 850-414-32399

STATE OF GEORGIA DEPARTMENT OF PUBLIC SAFETY
DRIVER SERVICES DIVISION
959 East Confederate Avenue SE, Atlanta, GA 30316
Phone: 404-657-9300

HAWAII MOTOR VEHICLE SAFETY OFFICE
1505 Dillingham Boulevard, Honolulu, HI 96817
Phone: 808-832-5820

IDAHO TRANSPORTATION DEPARTMENT
DIVISION OF MOTOR VEHICLES
P.O. Box 7129, Boise, ID 83707-1129
Phone: 208-334-8000

ILLINOIS MOTORIST SERVICES
VEHICLE SERVICES DEPARTMENT
RECORD INQUIRY SECTION
501 South 2nd Street, Springfield, IL 62756
Phone: 217-237-3202

INDIANA BUREAU OF MOTOR VEHICLES
100 North Senate Avenue, Room N440, Indianapolis, In 46204
Phone: 317-233-2349

IOWA DEPARTMENT OF TRANSPORTATION
MOTOR VEHICLE DIVISION
P.O. Box 9204, De Moines, IA 50306
Phone: 515-237-3202

KANSAS DEPARTMENT OF REVENUE
DIVISION OF MOTOR VEHICLES
Sheila Walker, Topeka, KS 66626-0001
Phone: 913-296-3660

KENTUCKY DIVISION OF VEHICLE LICENSING
TITLE BRANCH
P.O. Box 2014, Frankfort, KY 40602
Phone: 502-564-5301

LOUISIANA OFFICE OF MOTOR VEHICLES
P.O. Box 64886, Baton Rouge, LA 70896
Phone: 504-925-6335

MAINE BUREAU OF MOTOR VEHICLES
SECRETARY OF STATE
29 State House Station, Augusta, ME 04333-0029
Phone: 207-351-4500

MARYLAND MOTOR VEHICLE ADMINISTRATION
6601 Ritchie Highway, Glen Burnie, MD 21062
Phone: 410-768-7274

MASSACHUSETTS REGISTRY OF MOTOR VEHICLES
P.O. Box 199100, Boston, MA 02119-9100
Phone: 617-351-4500

MICHIGAN DEPARTMENT OF STATE
DRIVER AND VEHICLE RECORDS
7064 Crowner Drive, Lansing, MI 48918
Phone: 517-322-1000

MINNESOTA DEPARTMENT OF PUBLIC SAFETY
DRIVER AND VEHICLE SERVICES
445 Minnesota Street, St. Paul, MN 55101
Phone: 612-296-9525

MISSISSIPPI DRIVER SERVICES BUREAU
P.O. Box 958, Jackson, MS 39205
Phone: 601-987-1200

MISSOURI DEPARTMENT OF MOTOR VEHICLES
P.O. Box 629, Jefferson City, MO 65105
Phone: 573-751-4509

MONTANA MOTOR VEHICLE DIVISION
P.O. Box 201430, 303 North Roberts, Helena, MY 59620
Phone: 406-444-4536

NEBRASKA DEPARTMENT OF MOTOR VEHICLES
301 Centennial Mall South, Lincoln, NE 68509
Phone: 402-471-2281
TDD: 402-471-4154

NEVADA DEPARTMENT OF MOTOR VEHICLES
AND PUBLIC SAFETY
555 Wright Way, Carson City, NV 89711-0400
Phone: 702-687-5505

NEW HAMPSHIRE TAXATION & REVENUE DEPARTMENT
MOTOR VEHICLE DIVISION
P.O. Box 1028, Joseph Montoya Building, Santa Fe, NM 87504-1028
Phone: 1-888-MVD-INFO

NEW JERSEY MOTOR VEHICLE SERVICES
225 East State Street, CN 160, Trenton, NJ 08666
Phone: 1-888-486-3339
TDD: 609-292-5120

NEW MEXICO TAXATION & REVENUE DEPARTMENT
MOTOR VEHICLE DIVISION
P.O. Box 1028, Joseph Montoya Building, Santa Fe, NM 87504-1028
Phone: 1-888-MVD-INFO

NEW YORK STATE DEPARTMENT OF MOTOR VEHICLES
6 Empire State Plaza, Albany, NY 12229
Upstate: 1-800-CALL-DMV
516, 914 area: 1-800-DIAL-DMV
212 area 645-5550, Spanish: 645-4465
718 area 966-6155, Spanish: 966-6230

NORTH CAROLINA DIVISION OF MOTOR VAHICLES
1100 Raleigh Bern Avenue, Raleigh, NC 27697
Phone: (919) 715-7000

NORTH DAKOTA DRIVER'S LICENSE AND TRAFFIC SAFETY DIVISION
608 East Boulevard Avenue, Bismarck, ND 58505-0700
Phone: 701-328-2725

OHIO BUREAU OF MOTOR VEHICLES
1970 West Broad Street, Columbus, Ohio 43223
Phone: 614-752-7600
TDD: 614-752-7681

OKLAHOMA DEPARTMENT OF PUBLIC SAFETY ACCIDENT RECORDS DIVISION
3600 North Martin Luther King Boulevard, Oklahoma City, OK 73111
Phone: 405-425-2000

OREGON DRIVER & MOTOR VEHICLE SERVICES BRANCH
1905 Lana Avenue, Salem, OR 97314
Phone: 503-945-5000

PENNSYLVANIA DEPARTMENT OF TRANSPORTATION DRIVER AND VEHICLE SERVICES
1101-1125 South Front Street, Harrisburg, PA 17104
Phone: 717-391-6190

RHODE ISLAND MOTOR VEHICLES
286 Main Street, Paw tucker, RI 02869
Phone: 401-277-2970, ext. 2039

SOUTH CAROLINA DIVISION OF MOTOR VEHICLES
P.O. Box 1498, Columbia, SC 29216
Phone: 803-737-1654

SOUTH DAKOTA DEPARTMENT OF REVENUE
DIVISION OF MOTOR VEHICLES
445 East Capital Avenue, Pierre, SD 57501-3185
Phone: 605-773-5335

TENNESSEE DEPARTMENT OF SAFETY
DRIVER LICENSE ISSUANCE DIVISION
1150 Foster Avenue, Nashville, Tennessee 37249-1000
Phone: 615-741-3954
TTD: 615-532-1181

TEXAS DEPARTMENT OF TRANSPORTATION
CORRESPONDENCE SECTION
P.O. Box 12098, Austin, TX 78711-2098
Phone: 512-465-6711

THE UTAH DRIVER LICENSE DIVISION
4501 South 2700 West, Salt Lake City, Utah 84119
Phone: 801-965-4437

STATE OF VERMONT DEPARTMENT OF MOTOR VEHICLES
State Office Building, 120 State Street, Montpelier, Vermont 05601
Phone: 802-828-2000

VIRGINIA DEPARTMENT OF MOTOR VEHICLES
P.O. Box 17412, Richmond, VA 23269
Phone: 804-367-0538 (Richmond & vicinity)
Phone: 757-461-1919 (Tidewater)
Phone: 804-309-1500 (Western Virginia)
Phone: 703-761-4655 (Northern Virginia)

WASHINGTON DEPARTMENT OF LICENSING

1125 Washington Street, SE, P.O. Box 9020, Olympia,
WA 98507-9020
Phone: 360-902-3600
TDD 360-664-8885

WEST VIRGINIA DIVISION OF MOTOR VEHICLES

1800 Kanawha Boulevard East, Charleston, WV 25317
Phone: 1-800-558-9066

WISCONSIN DIVISION OF MOTOR VEHICLES

P.O. Box 7918, Madison 53707-7918
Phone: 608-266-1466

WYOMING DEPARTMENT OF TRANSPORTATION
DRIVER SERVICES DIVISION

P.O. Box 1708, Cheyenne, WY 82003-1708
Phone: 307-777-4800

NOTES: _____

_____

_____

_____

_____

_____

_____

_____

_____

_____

_____

_____

_____

_____

_____

_____

Agencies
& Organizations

Usefull Agencies and Contacts –

Including Dealer Floor Plan Sources

AGENCIES AND/OR ORGANIZATIONS

ADESA - CORPORATION
Two Parkwood Crossing, 310 East 96th Street, Suite 400
Indianapolis, IN 46240
Phone: 317-815-1100
Fax: 317-862-7231
www.adesaauctions.com

ADESA CANADA, INC.
1717 Burton Road, Vars, Ontario KOA 3HO
Phone: 613-443-4400
Fax: 613-443-0423

ADT AUTOMOTIVE, INC.
435 Metroplex Drive, Nashville, TN 37211
Phone: 615-781-3194
Executive Fax: 615-781-3194
Accounting Fax: 615-837-7814
Remarketing Fax: 615-837-7806
Sales Fax: 615-781-3273
Advertising Fax: 615-837-7810
Legal Fax: 615-781-3277
Administrative Fax: 615-781-3277
www.adtauto.com

AUCTION FINANCE GROUP

1680 Michigan Avenue, Suite 701, Miami Beach, FL 33139
Phone: 888-843-3562
Fax: 800-881-2400
www.floor-plan.com

BSCAMERICA AUCTION GROUP

803 Belair Road, Bel Air, MD 21014
Phone: 905-791-9800
Fax: 905-791-4200
www.cag.com

CANADIAN AUCTION GROUP

3365 Highway #7 East, Brampton, Ontario L6T 5P4
Phone: 410-879-7950
Fax: 410-879-9993
www.bscamerica.com

MANHEIM'S LOUISVILLE AUTO AUCTION

5425 Highway 31 East, Clarksville, IN 47129
Phone: 812-283-0734
Fax: 812-280-8458

MANHEIM AUCTIONS

1400 Lake Hearn Drive, N.E., Clarkesville, IN 47129
Phone: 812-283-0734
Fax: 812-280-8458
www.manheim.com

THE AUCTION FINANCE PROGRAM

1680 Michigan Avenue, Miami Beach, FL 33139
Phone: 888-843-3562
Fax: 800-881-2400
www.floor-plan.com

AUCTION INSURANCE AGENCY, INC.
2200 Woodcrest Place, Birmingham, AL 35209
Phone: 205-877-4500
Fax: 205-877-4515
www.auctioninsurance.com

AUCTION PHONE SERVICE
1367 Anita Street, Grosse Pointe, MI 48236
Phone: 313-343-6473

AUCTION SOFTWARE, INC.
220 Water Street, 2nd Floor, Statesville, NC 28677
Phone: 704-872-2458
Fax: 704-873-6119
www.aucsoft.com

AUTO AUCTION SERVICES CORPORATION
629 Green Bay Road, Suite 4, Wilmette, IL 60091
Phone: 847-256-6729
Fax: 847-256-6759
www.aascend.com

AUTO LENDERS ACCEPTANCE CORPORATION
300 Interstate North Parkway, 6th Floor, Atlanta, GA 30339
Phone: 770-956-3800
Fax: 800-959-3975

AUTO MAGIC/AWC
1275 Round Table Drive, Dallas, TX 75247
Phone: 800-826-0828
Fax: 214-634-1342
www.autowaxcompany.com

AUTOMOTIVE FINANCE CORP. (AFC)
Two Parkwood Crossing, 310 East 96th Street, Suite 300,
Indianapolis, IN 46240
Phone: 317-815-9645
Fax: 317-815-9650

AUTOMOTIVE MARKET REPORT
1713 Ardmore Boulevard, Pittsburgh, PA 15221-4477
Phone: 412-242-3900
Fax: 412-242-7033

AUTOMOTIVE NEWS
1400 Woodbridge Avenue, Detroit, MI 48207
Phone: 313-446-6065
Fax: 313-446-8030

AUTO USE
45 Haverhill Street, Andover, MA 01810
Phone: 508-475-4883
Fax: 508-470-2721

BLACK BOOK
2620 Barrett Road, Gainesville, GA 30507
Phone: 770-532-4111
Fax: 770-532-4792
www.blackbookguides.com

CARFAX, INC.
3975 Fair Ridge Drive, Suite 200, North Fairfax, VA 22033-2924
Phone: 703-934-2664
Fax: 703-273-5194

DAIMLER-CHRYSLER CORPORATION
Vehicle Remarketing, 27777 Franklin Road, 20th Floor,
Southfield, MI 48034
Phone: 248-948-3626

DENT WIZARD INTERNATIONAL CORPORATION
3003 S. Hanley Road, St. Louis, MO 63143
Phone: 314-645-0004
Fax: 314-645-2612

ENTERPRISE RENT-A-CAR
600 Corporate Park Drive, St. Louis, MO 63105
Phone: 314-512-5000
Fax: 314-512-4931 or 314-512-4582
www.pickenterprise.com

FORD MOTOR COMPANY
Regent Court Building, 16800 Executive Drive, Mail Drop 6N-2A,
Dearborn, MI 48126 Phone: 313-621-6118

FLOOR PLAN SOURCES FOR DEALERS

Money to Purchase Your Inventory

FLOOR PLAN SOURCES FOR DEALERS
Money to Purchase Your Inventory

AFC - AUTOMOTIVE FINANCE CORP.
310 E. 96th St., Suite 300, Indianapolis, IN 46240
Phone: 407-328-1522
www.afcdealer.com

MAFS - Manheim Auto Financial Services
Atlanta, GA
www.usemafs.com

WELLS FARGO SMALL BUSINESS
www.wellsfargo.com/biz

GMAS FINANCIAL SERVICES
www.gmacfs.com

GE CAPITAL FLEET SERVICES
3 Capital Drive, Eden Prairie, MN 55344
Phone: 612-828-2116
Fax: 612-828-2321

GENERAL MOTORS ACCEPTANCE CORP. (GMAC)
3044 West Grand Boulevard, Mail CodeL 482-102-154
Detroit, MI 48202
Phone: 313-556-0500
Fax: 313-974-4614

GENERAL MOTORS CORPORATION
GM Auction Department, 100 Renaissance Center,
Mail Code: 482-A11-D46, Detroit, MI 48265-1000
Phone: 313-667-9496
Fax: 313-667-9393

THE HERTZ CORPORATION
225 Brue Boulevard, Oark Edge, NJ 07656
Phone: 201-307-2696

THE INSURANCE EXCHANGE, INC.
751 Rockville Pike, Suite 3A, Rockville, MD 20852
Phone: 301-279-5500
Fax: 301-424-2829

KELLEY BLUE BOOK
5 Oldfield, Irvine, CA 92618
Phone: 949-770-7704
Fax: 949-329-1019
www.kbb.com

MENDENHALL SCHOOL OF AUCTIONEERING
6729 Auction Road, Archdale, NC 27263
Phone: 336-887-1165
Fax: 336-887-1107

MERCEDES-BENZ CREDIT CORPORATION
7 Village Circle, Suite 300, Roanoke, TX 75063
Phone: 817-430-5400
Fax: 817-430-5593

N/S VEHICLE WASH SYSTEMS
235 West Florence Avenue, Inglewood, CA 90301
Phone: 310-412-7074
Fax: 310-673-0276

NADA OFFICIAL USED CAR GUIDE CO.
8400 Westpark Drive, McLean, VA 22102
Phone: 800-544-6232
Fax: 703-821-7269

NATIONAL MARKET REPORTS

29 North Wacker Drive, 9th Floor, Chicago, IL 60606-3297
Phone: 312-726-2802
Fax: 312-855-0137

NIADA'S USED CAR DEALER MAGAZINE

2521 Brown Boulevard, Arlington, TX 76006
Phone: 817-640-3838
Fax: 817-649-5866

REMARKETING SERVICES OF AMERICA, INC.

40 John Glenn Drive, Suite 100, Amherst, NY 14228
Phone: 716-564-4000
Fax: 716-564-4040

TOYOTA MOTOR CREDIT/LEXUS FINANCIAL SERVICES

19001 South Western Avenue, Torrance, CA 90509
Phone: 310-787-3745
Fax: 310-787-3502

VOLKSWAGEN CREDIT/AUDI FINANCIAL SEVICES

3800 Hamlin Road, Auburn Hills, MI 48326
Phone: 248-340-5388
Fax: 248-340-5029

WHEELS, INC.

666 garland Place, Des Plaines, IL 60016
Phone: 847-699-7000
Fax: 847-699-9470

WORLD OMNI FINANCIAL CORPORATION

120 N.W. 12th Avenue, Deerfield Beach, FL 33442
Phone: 954-429-2000
Fax: 954-429-2299

Dealer
Auto
Auctions

You're Personal Guide, to connect you to all the Major Auto Auctions throughout the Nation.

Auctions - Dealer and Public are Listed Alphabetically by State.

YOUR LOCAL CONTACTS

ie. Local car dealers, detail shops, mechanics, Neighborhood auctions

NAME   **ADDRESS**   **PHONE**

_____

_____

_____

_____

_____

_____

_____

_____

Although this contact booklet has a lot of major contacts, you will also want to fill in alot of local contacts of your own

AUTO NEWS SUBSCRIPTIONS

Used Car News
24840 Harper
St. Clair Shores, MI 48080

Phone - 810-772-5200
Fax - 810-772-9400
Toll Free - 800-794-0760
Web - eusedcarnews.com

Automotive News
PO Box 07915
Detroit, MI 48207-9902

Auto Remarketing
1150 SE Maryland Road
Suite 210
North Carolina 27511

Phone - 919-469-9911
Fax - 919-481-2658

AUTO DEALER VALUE GUIDES

Black Book
PO Box 758
Gainesville, GA 30503-0758

Phone - 1-800-554-1026
Fax - 800-357-3444

NADA
8400 Westpark Drive
Mc Lean, VA 22102-9985
NADAGUIDE.COM

CPI
(Cars of Particular Interest)
PO Box 3190
Laurel, MD 20709

1-800-927-5312

AUCTION LOCATIONS

ALABAMA
ADESA - Birmingham
804 Sollie Drive, Moody, AL 35004
Phone: 205-640-1010
Fax: 205-640-1024
www.adesaauctions.com

Auto Auction of Montgomery
6044 Troy Highway, Montgomery, AL 26116
Phone: 334-288-3399
Fax: 334-288-7330

Boyette Brothers Auction
Attn: Tanya Jackson, Montgomery Police Department
320 North Ripley, Montgomery, AL 36104
Phone: 334-241-2762

Center Point Auction
100 13th Court, N.E., Birmingham, AL 35215
Phone: 205-856-6527
Fax: 205-856-6538

Dealers Auto Auction, Inc. of Huntsville
26125 U.S. Highway 72, East Athens, AL 35611
Phone: 256-232-0201
Fax: 256-232-8822

Dothan Auto Auction
3664 South Oates Street, Dothan, AL 36301
Phone: 334-792-1115
Fax: 334-671-9556
www.adtauto.com

Insurance Auto Auctions
16326 Ennis Road, Athens, AL 35611
Phone: 205-233-5899
Fax: 205-233-2366
www.home.iaai.com

Insurance Auto Auctions
1600 Highway 150, Bessemer, AL 35022
Phone: 205-426-2300
Fax: 205-428-5332 www.home.iaai.com

Kelly Auto Auction
Boaz Highway, Attalla, AL 35954
Phone: 205-538-9095

Kirby Auto Brokers
203 Oakwood Avenue, NE, Huntsville, AL 35811-1965
Phone: 205-539-2001

Oxford Auto Auction
2344 Highway 21 South, Anniston, AL 36203-2907
Phone: 205-835-2158

ARIZONA

Arizona Auto Auction
3420 South 48th Street, Phoenix, AZ 85040
Phone: 602-894-2400
Fax: 602-894-0938
www.manheim.com

Barrett-Jackson: Classic Car Auction WestWorld of Scottsdale
16601 North Pima Road, Scottsdale, AZ 85258
www.barrett-jackson.com

ADOT Public Auctions Arizona Department of Transportation
2350 South 22nd Avenue, Phoenix, AZ 85000
Phone: 602-712-6505
www.dot.state.az.us/about/equipsvcs/index.htm

Dealers Insurance Auto Auctions
2299 W. Broadway Road, Phoenix, AZ 85041
Phone: 602-243-2731
Fax: 602-268-5242
www.home.iaai.com

Manheim's Greater Auto Auction of Phoenix
200 North 83rd Avenue, Phoenix, AZ 85043
Phone: 602-907-7000
Fax: 602-907-7066
www.manheim.com

Manheim's Tucson Auto Auction
7090 South Cray croft Road, Tucson, AZ 85706
Phone: 502-574-2222
Fax: 520-574-2554

New Phoenix Auto Auction
8833 North Black Canyon Highway, Phoenix, AZ 85021-4107
Phone: 602-395-9092

Southwest Auto Auction
400 N. Beck Avenue, Chandler, AZ 85526
Phone: 602-961-1161
Fax: 602-921-9008
www.manheim.com

Sunburst Car Company, Arizona's #1 Public Auto Auction
3777 NW Grand Avenue, Phoenix, AZ 85019-3408
Phone: 602-246-2353
Fax: 602-246-8085
www.sunburstcarco.com

Western Sales Auctioneers
1616 So. 67th Avenue, Phoenix, AZ 85043-7700
Phone: 602-936-3300

ARKANSAS
Central Arkansas Auto Auction, Inc.
162 Highway 64W, Beebe, AR 72012-0250
Phone: 501-882-0250
Fax: 501-882-6718

Mid-Ark Auto Auction
8700 Highway 70, North Little Rock, AR 72117
Phone: 501-945-2444
Fax: 501-945-7985

Paragould Auto Auction
2401 Highway 49 North, Paragould, AR 72450
Phone: 501-239-9504
Fax: 501-239-9091

CALIFORNIA
ADESA-Sacramento
8649 Kiefer Boulevard, Sacramento, CA 95826
Phone: 916-388-8899
Fax: 916-388-0838
www.adesaauctions.com

Alameda County Auction
6438 Sierra Court, Dublin, CA 94568
Phone: 510-929-5999
www.acauction.com

American West Investment Auto Auctioneers
28436 Satellite Street, Hayward, CA 94545-4863
Phone: 510-732-0267

Auction City
3536 Haven Avenue, Redwood City, CA 94063-4603
Phone: 650-367-7788
www.auctioncity.com

Auto Auction Group, Inc.
2242 San Fernando Road, Los Angeles, CA 90065
Phone: 213-222-8000

Bay Cities Auto Auction
29900 Auction Way, Hayward, CA 94544
Phone: 510-786-4500
Fax: 510-786-0745

Brusher's Sacramento Auto Auction
6233 Blacktop Road, Rio Linda, CA 95673
Phone: 916-991-5555
Fax: 916-991-5445
www.brashers.com

California Auto Dealers Exchange
1320 North Tustin Avenue, Anaheim, CA 92807
Phone: 714-996-2400
Fax: 714-996-9297
www.manheim.com

City of Long Beach
3111 E. Willow Street, Long Beach, CA 90806
Recorded Info: 562-570-2855
www.ci.long-beach.ca.us

County Public Auto Auction
3492 Burns Valley Road, Clearlake, CA 95422
Phone: 707-994-2886

Ernst Auction Park
824 Kiernan Avenue, Modesto, CA 95356
Phone: 209-527-7399
www.rogernst.com

Fairfield Auto & Truck Auction
1800 N Texas Street, Fairfield, CA 94533-3822
Phone: 707-425-3395

Friendly Auto Auction
14364 Santa Ana Avenue, Fontana, CA 92335
Phone: 909-355-7071

Golden Gate Auto Auction
6700 Stevenson Boulevard, Fremont, CA 94538
Phone: 510-657-5660
www.adtauto.com

Insurance Auto Auctions
2961 E. La Jolla Street, Anaheim, CA 92806
Phone: 714-630-5602
Fax: 714-630-8277
www.home.iaai.com/html/buyrlist.htm

Insurance Auto Auctions
2800 S. Trade Avenue, Colton, CA 92324
Phone: 909-784-2700
Fax: 909-784-5704
www.home.iaai.com/html/buyrlist.htm

Insurance Auto Auctions
4334 San Gabriel River Parkway, Pico Rivera, CA 90660
Phone: 562-699-9951
Fax: 562-699-0055
www.home.iaai.com/html/buyrlist.htm

Insurance Auto Auctions
10728 US Elevator Road, Suite 101, Spring Valley, CA 91978
Phone: 619-670-1400
Fax: 619-670-9652
www.home.iaai.com/html/buyrlist.htm

Insurance Auto Auctions
400 E. Redondo Beach Road, Suite A, Gardena, CA 90248
Phone: 310-323-3330
Fax: 310-323-6625
www.home.iaai.com/html/buyrlist.htm

Insurance Auto Auctions
400 E. Redondo Beach Road, Suite A, Gardena, CA 90248
Phone: 818-786-2200
Fax: 818-765-4561
www.home.iaai.com/html/buyrlist.htm

Insurance Auto Auctions
13901 San Bernardino Avenue, Fondant, CA 92335
Phone: 909-355-9400
Fax: 909-822-9311
www.home.iaai.com/html/buyrlist.htm

Insurance Auto Auctions
7245 Laurel Canyon Boulevard, North Hollywood, CA 91605
Phone: 818-786-2200
Fax: 818-765-4561

Joe Bradley Auctioneers
2523 Marina Boulevard, San Diego, CA 92110
www.bestautoauctions.com

Ken Porter Auction Company
813 Garden Street, Santa Barbara, CA 93101
Phone: 805-966-0017
Fax: 805-966-7464
www.kpaco.com

L.A. Auto Auction
80001 Garvey Avenue, Rosemead, CA 91770-2477
Phone: 818-573-8001
Fax: 909-822-9311
www.home.iaai.com/html/buyrlist.htm

Los Angeles Dealer Auto Auction
8001 Garvey Avenue, Rosemead, CA 91770
Phone: 626-573-8001
Fax: 626-307-8283
www.manheim.com

Manheim's Fresno Auto Dealers Auction
278 North Marks, Fresno, CA 93706
Phone: 209-268-8051
Fax: 209-268-9491
www.home.iaai.com/html/buyrlist.htm

Mission City Auto Auction
2175 Cactus Road, San Diego, CA 92173
Phone: 619-661-5565
Fax: 619-661-5570

Nationwide Auction Systems
3901 S. Bennington Avenue, Kansas City, MO 64129
Phone: 816-861-7079
www.nationwideauction.com

Norwalk Auto Auction
12405 East Rosecrans Avenue, Norwalk, CA 90650
Phone: 562-864-7464
Fax: 562-863-2776

Oasis Auto Auction
1402 Heritage Road, San Yoshiro, CA 92173-1640
Phone: 619-661-6064

Orange County Main Public Auto Auction
4300 Westminster Avenue, Santa Ana, CA 92703-1313
Phone: 714-741-7565

Palm Springs Exotic Car Auction
602 E. Sunny Dunes Road, Palm Springs, CA 92264
Phone: 760-320-3290
Phone: 760-320-2850
Fax: 760-323-7031
www.classic-carauction.com

Riverside Auto Auction
6446 Fremont, Riverside, CA 92504
Phone: 909-689-6000
Fax: 909-689-5567
www.manheim.com

San Diego Auto Auction
4691 Calle Joven, Oceanside, CA 92057-6042
Phone: 760-754-3600
Fax: 760-754-3690
www.adtauto.com

Southern California Auto Auction
10700 Beech Avenue, Fontana, CA 92337-7217
Phone: 909-822-2261
Fax: 909-829-1370
www.manheim.com

Spectrum Auction Company
23291 Ventura Boulevard, Woodland Hills, CA 91364
Phone: 818-225-8828
Fax: 818-225-8848
www.spectrumauctions.com

COLORADO
Loveland Auto Auctions, Inc.
2500 East 13th Street, Loveland, CO 80536
Phone: 970-669-4994
Fax: 970-669-9874

Mr. CS Auto Auction
1315 West Quincy Avenue
Englewood, CO 80110-4411
Phone: 303-781-7357

Norwest Auto Auction
330 North Circle Drive, Colorado Springs, CO 80909-6249
Phone: 719-632-5420

Pacific Auction Companies
5450 Dahlia, Commerce City, CO 80022
Phone: 303-287-0691

CONNECTICUT
Greater New haven Auto Auction, Inc.
51 Longhini Lane, New haven, CT 06519
Phone: 203-771-1218
Fax: 203-772-1220

Newington Auto Auction, Inc.
181 Pane Road, Newington, CT 06111-5522
Phone: 203-666-5426

Southern Auto Auction
161-164 South Main Street, East Windsor, CT 06088-0388
Phone: 860-292-7500
Fax: 860-292-7597
www.southern-aa.com

DELAWARE
Delaware Auto Exchange
Route 13, P.O. Box 326, Felton, Delaware 19943
Phone: 302-284-8250
Fax: 302-284-8260

Diamond State Auto Auction
Route 13, Felton, Delaware 19943
Phone: 302-284-3906

FLORIDA
ADESA-Jacksonville
11700 New Kings Road, Jacksonville, FL 32219
904-764-1004
Fax: 904-768-0029
www.adesaauctions.com

ADESA-South Florida
12700 N.W. 42nd Avenue, Opa Locka, FL 33054
Phone: 305-685-6363
Fax: 305-685-9215
www.adesaauctions.com

A & M Auction & Auto
Woodville Highway, Tallahassee, FL 32301
Phone: 904-421-5046

Auto Dealers Exchange
6005 - 24th St. East, Bradenton, FL 34203

Bayside Auto Auction of Tampa
3225 North 50th Street, Tampa, FL 33619
Phone: 813-620-3600
Fax: 813-623-3280

Big Sun Auto Auction
1205 NW 27th Avenue, Ocala, FL 34475
Phone: 352-368-5900
Fax: 352-368-2051
www.autoinsider.com/bigsun

Capital City Auto Auction
1602 capital Circle SW, Tallahassee, FL 32310-9246
Phone: 904-878-6200
Fax: 353-368-2051
www.autoinsider.com/bigsun

Clearwater Auto Auction
5153 - 126th Avenue North, Clearwater, FL 33760
Phone: 727-573-3630
Fax: 727-573-1613
www.adtauto.com

Cocoa Auto Auction
500 Cox Road, Cocoa, FL 32925
Phone: 407-636-2886
Fax: 407-636-9212

Daytona Auto Dealers Exchange
1305 Indian Lake Road, Daytona Beach, FL 32124
Phone: 904-255-2500
Fax: 904-255-3501
www.manheim.com

Daytona Auto Auction, Inc.
3143 West International Speedway, Daytona Beach, FL 32124-1019
Phone: 904-255-8311
Fax: 904-255-3501
www.manheim.com

Dealers Auto Auction of Sanford Inc.
3895 State Road, 46 East, Sanford, FL 32771
Phone: 407-323-4090
Fax: 407-323-4557
www.adtauto.com

Florida Auto Auction of Orlando
11801 West Colonial Drive, Ocoee, FL 34761
Phone: 407-656-6200
Fax: 407-656-7846
www.manheim.com

Fort Pierce Auto Auction
4116 Saint Lucie Boulevard, Ft. Pierce, FL 34946
Phone: 561-460-6699

Fax: 561-461-1309
www.bscamerica.com

Greater Tampa Bay Auto Auction
401 South 50th Street, Tampa, FL 33619
Phone: 813-247-1666
Fax: 813-247-1714
www.manheim.com

Imperial Auto Auction
3300 County Line Road, Lakeland, FL 33811
Phone: 941-607-6000
Fax: 941-607-5441
www.manheim.com

Interstate Auction of Ocala
540 S.W. 38th Avenue, Ocala, FL 34474
Phone: 352-351-5100
Fax: 352-620-8955
www.manheim.com

Jacksonville Auto Auction
11982 New Kings Road, U.S. Route 1 North, Jacksonville, FL 32219
Phone: 904-764-7653
Fax: 904-764-9528
www.manheim.com

Lakeland Auto Auction
8025 North State Road 33, Lakeland, FL 33809
Phone: 941-984-1551
Fax: 941-984-3029

Lauderdale-Miami Auto Auction
5353 South State Road 7, Davie, FL 33314
Phone: 954-791-3520
Fax: 954-791-3522
www.adtauto.com

Manheim's Pensacola Auto Auction
401 West Burgess Road, Pensacola, FL 32503
Phone: 850-477-3063
Fax: 850-474-1255
www.manheim.com

Orlando Auto Auction
571 Mercy Drive, Orlando, FL 32805
Phone: 407-299-3904
Fax: 407-294-6982

Orlando Orange County Auction
151 Taft-Vineland Road, Orlando, FL 32824
Phone: 407-851-6656
Fax: 407-856-0420

Pasco County Auto Auction
11709 State Road, Port Richey, FL 34669-3088
Phone: 813-856-1771

The South Florida Auto Auction
3500 NW 21 Street, Lauderdale Lakes, FL 33311
Phone: 954-739-9996
www.sflaa.com

Southwest Florida Auto Auction
2100 Rockville Road, Ft. Meyers, FL 33902
Phone: 941-337-5141
Fax: 941-337-7711

Saint Pete Auto Action
2100 Rockville Road, Ft. Meyers, FL 33902
Phone: 727-531-7717
www.manheim.com

Tallahassee Auto Auction
160 Capital Circle, S.W., Tallahassee, FL 32310
Phone: 850-878-6200
Fax: 850-942-9830
www.bscamerica.com

West Palm Beach Auto Auction
600 Sainsbury Way, West Palm Beach, FL 33411
Phone: 561-790-1200
Fax: 561-798-0774
www.adtauto.com

GEORGIA

Albany Auto Auction, Inc.
1421 Liberty Expressway, SE, Albany, GA 31705
Phone: 912-435-7708
Fax: 912-888-8035

Atlanta Auto Auction
4900 Buffington Road, Red oak, GA 30272
Phone: 404-762-9211
Fax: 404-765-0143
www.manheim.com

Bishop Brothers Auto Auction
2244 Metropolitan Parkway SW, Atlanta, GA 30315
Phone: 404-767-3652
Fax: 404-766-2180
www.manheim.com

Calhoun Auto Auction
2236 Rome Road SW
Calhoun, GA 30701-3212
Phone: 706-629-8632
Fax: 404-766-2180

Georgia Dealers Auto Auction
7205 Campbell ton Road, Atlanta, GA 30331
Phone: 404-349-5555
Fax: 404-349-9951
www.manheim.com

Lamar Nash's Loganville Auto Auction
2970 Highway 78, Loganville, GA 30249-3711
Phone: 404-466-3711

Marietta Auto Auction
3355 North Cobb Parkway, Acworth, GA 30101-3940
Phone: 404-974-8134

Oakwood's Arrow Auto Auction, Inc.
4712 Flat Creek Road, Oakwood, GA 30566-3101
Phone: 404-532-4624

Peary's Auto Auction, Inc.
628 South Main Street, Swainsboro, GA 30401
Phone: 912-237-8270
Fax: 912-237-6716

Reeds Auto Sales & Auction
1952 Chatsworth Highway, #255 North, Calhoun,
GA 30701-8402
Phone: 706-625-5684

Rome Auto Auction
Highway 411 North, Kingston, GA 30145
Phone: 404-336-5581

Southern Aucnet USA, Inc.
900 Circle 75, Parkway Suite 400, Atlanta, GA 30339
Phone: 800-428-2638
www.aucnet.com/index01.htm

Southern States Vehicle Auction
300 Raymond Hill Road, Newnan, GA 30265
Phone: 770-251-9881
Fax: 770-251-9928
www.adtauto.com

Wrights Auto Auction
2236 Rome Road Southwest, Calhoun, GA 30701-3212
Phone: 706-629-8632

HAWAII
Aloha Auto Auction
Kapalama Military Reservation, Building 905, Honolulu, HI 96816
Phone: 808-847-1799
Fax: 808-847-2438

IDAHO
Idaho Auto Auction
7355 South Eisenman Road, Boise, ID 83716

Phone: 208-345-7345
Fax: 208-395-3138
www.idaa.com

Musick & Sons Auctioneers, Inc.
1445 E. State Street, eagle, ID 83616
Phone: 208-939-1777
www.musick-auction.com

Treasure Valley Auto Auction
6724 Cleveland Boulevard, Caldwell, ID 83605
Phone: 208-454-0117

IILLINOIS
ADE (Auto Dealers Exchange) of Illinois
43363 North Old Highway 41, Russell, IL 60075-0100
Phone: 847-395-7570 Fax: 847-395-7479

Arena Auto Auction, Inc.
200 West Old Chicago Drive, Bolingbrook, IL 60440
Phone: 630-759-3800
Fax: 630-759-9668
www.adtauto.com

Auction Way Sales
12000 South Cicero Avenue, Alsip, IL 60803-2313
Phone: 708-597-3345
Fax: 708-597-4003
www.manheim.com

Chicago Suto Auction
4030 North Rockwell Street, Chicago, IL 60618
Phone: 773-267-0999

Decatur Auto Auction
1991 West Mound Road, Decatur, IL 62526
Phone: 217-875-4220
Fax: 217-875-2927

Gateway Auto Auction
440 West Pontoon Road, Granite City, IL 62040
Phone: 618-451-7675
Fax: 618-451-6912
www.manheim.com

Greater Chicago Auto Auction
12161 South Central, Chicago, IL 60658
Phone: 708-597-3600
Fax: 708-597-1692
www.manheim.com

Greater Rockford Auto Auction
5937 Sandy Hollow Road, Rockford, IL 61109
Phone: 815-874-7800
Fax: 815-874-1325

Mid City Auto Auctions Sales
7641 South Ashland Avenue, Chicago, IL 60620
Phone: 773-487-5900

Tri-State Auto Auction
9197 North IL Route 84, Galena, IL 61036

Phone: 815-777-1147
Fax: 309-266-5414

Tri-State Auto Auction
4740 West 135th Street, Crestwood, IL 60445
Phone: 708-389-4488
Fax: 708-389-4558

Valley Auto Auction
Route 51 South, Clinton, Illinois 61727
Phone: 217-935-8211
Fax: 217-935-3795
www.martinauction.com

INDIANA
ADE (Auto Dealers Exchange)
8800 Brooksville Road, Indianapolis, IN 46239
Phone: 317-352-0121
Fax: 317-356-6597
www.martinauction.com

ADESA-Indianapolis
2950 East Main Street, Plainfield, IN 46168
Phone: 317-838-8000
Fax: 317-838-8081
www.adesaauctions.com

ADESA-Indianapolis
11490 U.S. 31 North, Edinburgh, IN 46124
Phone: 812-526-9731
Fax: 812-526-9734
www.adesaauctions.com

Alexandria Public Auto Auction
S R 9 Alexandria Drive, Alexandria, IN 46001
Phone: 371-724-7653
Fax: 812-526-9734
www.adesaauctions.com

Austin Public Auto Auction
York Road, Austin, IN 47102-1448
Phone: 812-794-2588
Fax: 812-526-9734

Fort Wayne Vehicle Auction, Inc.
3600 east Washington Boulevard, Fort Wayne, IN 46803
Phone: 219-422-9577
Fax: 219-422-3409
www.adtauto.com

Indiana Auto Auction, Inc.
4425 West Washington Center Rd., Fort Wayne, IN 46818
Phone: 219-489-2776
Fax: 219-489-5476

Indianapolis Car Exchange
5161 S. Indianapolis Rd., Suite A, Whites town, IN 46075
Phone: 317-769-7777
Fax: 317-769-7070

Indy Public Auto Auction
2260 West Main Street, Greenfield, IN 46140-2717
Phone: 317-467-4700

Kessler Schaefer Auto Auction, Inc.
5333 West 46th Street, Indianapolis, IN 46254
Phone: 317-297-2300
Fax: 317-297-6234

Kruse International
5540 County Road 11-A, Auburn, Indiana 46706
Phone: 800-968-4444
Fax: 219-925-5467

Mid States Auto Auction
25784 Western Avenue, South Bend, IN 46619
Phone: 219-289-7767
Fax: 219-288-2731

Mishawaka Auto Auction
1209 east McKinley, Mishawaka, IN 46545
Phone: 219-256-5626
Fax: 219-256-5655

Wolfe's Terre Haute Auto Auction
1601 Margaret Avenue, Terre Haute, IN 47802
Phone: 812-238-1431
Fax: 812-235-6257

Wolfe's Evansville Auto Auction Inc.
2229 South Kentucky Avenue, Evansville, IN 47714
Phone: 812-425-4576
Fax: 812-425-4570

IOWA

Dealer's Choice Auto Auction
503 South Wapello Road, Mediapolis, IA 52637
Phone: 319-394-3510
Fax: 319-394-3511

Des Moines Auto Auction, Inc.
1530 east McKinley Avenue, Des Moines, IA 50320
Phone: 515-285-8911
Fax: 515-285-6905

Plaza Auto Auction
320 Highway 30 West, Mt. Vernon, IA 52314
Phone: 319-895-6232
Fax: 319-895-6727

KANSAS

I-70 Auto Auction
Interstate 70 & Valencia, Topeka, KS 66615
Phone: 913-478-4250

Mid-America Auto Auction
4716 South Santa Fe, Wichita, KS 67216
Phone: 316-522-8195
Fax: 316-522-8194

Mid-America Exotic Auto Sales
7801 West 63rd Terrace, Shawnee Mission, KS 66202-3808
Phone: 913-384-1717

Salina Auto Auction
Building 131 Forbes Field, Topeka, KS 66619

Phone: 785-862-1722
Fax: 785-862-1732

KENTUCKY
ADESA-Lexington
672 Blue Sky Parkway, Lexington, KY 40509
Phone: 606-263-5163
Fax: 606-263-5693 www.adesaauctions.com

Back's Auto Auction & Sales
1281 Winchester Road, Mount Sterling, KY 40353
Phone: 606-498-6373
Fax: 606-498-0538

Bowling Breen Auto Auction
565 Greenwood Lane, Bowling Green, KY 42014
Phone: 502-781-2422
Fax: 502-781-5362

Halls Westside Auto Auction & Sales
1877 Winchester Road, Mount Sterling, KY 40353-9727
Phone: 606-498-1414

Louisville Auto Auction, Inc.
5425 Highway 31 East, Clarksville, IN 47129
Phone: 812-283-0734
Fax: 812-283-5852

Mid-America Auto Auction
3515 Newburg Road, Louisville, KY 40218
Phone: 502-454-6666
Fax: 502-456-2919
Fax: 502-452-9518

Paducah Auto Auction, Inc.
2240 Bridge Street, Paducah, KY 42003
Phone: 502-442-9197

LOUISIANA
ADESA-Ark-La-Tex
7666 Highway 80 West, Shreveport, LA 71119
Phone: 800-264-7253
Fax: 318-938-7623
www.adesaauctions.com

Auto Auction of New Orleans
6600 Almonaster Avenue, New Orleans, A 70126
Phone: 504-242-9318
Fax: 504-242-9670

Dealers Auto Auction, Inc.
136 Gregory Drive, Monroe, LA 71202
Phone: 318-343-8200
Fax: 318-343-8259

Henderson Auctions
P.O. Box 336, Livingston, LA 70754
Phone: 504-686-2252
Fax: 504-686-7658

Manheim's Baton Rouge Auto Auction, Inc.
3609 Highway 1 North, Port Allen, LA 70767
Phone 504-343-2722
Fax: 504-343-2984
www.manheim.com

Manheim's Greater New Orleans Auto Auction
61077 Tammany Avenue, Slidell, LA 70460
Phone: 504-643-2061
Fax: 504-643-5657
www.manheim.com

Manheim's Lafayette Auto Auction
1611 Saint Mary Street, Highway 93, Scott, LA 70583
Phone: 318-237-5620
Fax: 318-237-0762
www.manheim.com

Shreveport Auto Auction Inc.
1315 Grimmett Drive, Shreveport, LA 71107-6501
Phone: 318-222-5784

MAINE
Acadia Auto Auction
RR 2, Box 4240, Carmel, ME 04419
Phone: 207-234-4444
Fax: 207-848-2010

Auto Auction of New England, Inc.
53 West Gray Road, Gray, ME 04419
Phone: 207-657-5800
Fax: 207-657-5802

Owls Head Transportation Auction
Route 73, Owls Head, Maine 04854
Phone: 207-594-4418
www.ohtm.org

Port City Auto Auction
County Road, Route 197, Richmond, ME 04357
Phone: 207-737-8331
Fax: 207-737-8346

MARYLAND
Auto Auction of Bel Air, Inc.
803 Bel Air Road, US Route 1, Bel Air, MD 21014
Phone: 410-879-7950 or 410-838-5880
Fax: 410-893-1515
www.bscamerica.com

Auto Plaza Marty Salins
15557 Frederick Road # D, Deerwood, MD 20855-2115
Phone: 301-340-1390

Baltimore-Washington Auto Exchange, Inc.
7151 Brook dale Drive, Elkridge, MD 21075
Phone: 410-796-8899
Fax: 410-700-0512
www.adtauto.com

Express Auction
3646 Falls Road, Baltimore, MD 21211
Phone: 410-243-9999
Fax: 410-243-1246
www.expressauction.com

PA Ave. Auto & Truck Auction, Inc.
9011 Dower House Road, Marlboro, MD 20772-4384
Phone: 301-599-0909

Penn Ave. Public Auto & Truck Auction
9011 Dower House Road, Upper Marlboro, MD 20772
Phone: 301-599-0909
www.pennave-autoauction.com

R.C. Bruckheimer & Associates
Maryland Route 40, North East, North East, MD 21901
Phone: 410-287-5588 or 1-800-233-4169
Fax: 410-287-2029
www.burkheimer.com

United Auto Auction Corporation
25 Proctor Street, Boston, MA 02119
Phone: 617-427-5700
Fax: 617-427-6216
www.quickpage.com

MASSACHUSETTS
ADESA-Boston
63 Western Avenue, Framingham, MA 01701
Phone: 508-626-7000
Fax: 508-626-7111
www.adesaauctions.com

American Auto Auction
123 Williams Street, North Dighton, MA 02764
Phone: 508-823-6600
Fax: 508-823-0006
www.manheim.com

Central Mass Auto Auction
22 Town Forrest Road, Oxford, MA 01540
Phone: 508-987-8396
Fax: 508-987-6430

Quincy Auto Auction
196 Riccuiti Drive, Quincy, MA 02169
Phone: 617-773-5000 Fax: 617-376-0997

MICHIGAN
ADESA-Lansing
6956 Lansing Road, Dimondale, MI 48821
Phone: 517-322-2444
Fax: 517-646-9160
www.adesaauctions.com

Bay Auto Auction
573 South Tuscola Road, Bay City, MI 48708
Phone: 517-891-9570
Fax: 517-891-9575
www.adesaauctions.com

Detroit Auto Auction, Inc.
20911 Gladwin, Taylor, MI 48180
Phone: 734-285-7300
Fax: 734-285-2025
www.adtauto.com

Flint Auto Auctions Inc.
3711 Western Road, Flint, MI 48506-2385
Phone: 810-736-2700
Fax: 810-736-3351
www.flintaa.com

Galvanek's Auto Auction
Phone: 616-862-3549
www.members.aol.com/galvaneks/index/html

Grand Rapids Auto Auction
2380 Port Sheldon Court, Jenison, MI 49428
Phone: 616-669-1050
Fax: 616-669-5522

Greater Kalamazoo Auto Auction
900 North U.S. 131, Schoolcraft, MI 49087
Phone: 616-679-5021
Fax: 616-679-4582
www.adtauto.com

Kingston Auto Auction
23 Don Street, Kingston, MI 48239
Phone: 613-577-8887 or 888-345-9100
www.redwing.on.ca/kbd.busdir/b3666.html

Manheim's Metro Detroit Auto Auction
29500 Gateway Drive, Flat Rock, MI 48134
Phone: 734-783-3799
Fax: 734-379-2528
www.manheim.com

Midwest Auto Auction
14666 Telegraph Road, Redford, MI 48239
Phone: 888-345-9100 or 313-538-2100
www.midwesternautoauction.com

Richmond Auto Auction
10788 Gratiot Avenue, Casco, MI 48064-1006
Phone: 810-727-4114

Tri-City Auto Auction
573 South Tuscola Road, Bay City, MI 48708-9632
Phone: 517-892-7355

West Michigan Auto Auction
4758 Division, Moline, MI 49335
Phone: 616-877-2020
Fax: 616-877-2040

MINNESOTA

Auto Dealers Exchange of Minneapolis, LLC
18270 Territorial Road, Daytona, MN 55369
Phone: 612-428-8777
Fax: 612-428-8701

Mid-America Collector Care and Motorcycles
2277 West Highway 36, Suite 214, Saint Paul, MN 55113
Phone: 612-633-9655
Fax: 612-633-3212
www.mm.com/swapmeet/auctions/midamer.htm

Mid-State Auto Auction
200 East Centennial Drive, New York Mills, MN 56567
Phone: 218-385-3777
Fax: 218-385-3232

Minneapolis Auto Auction
8001 Jefferson Highway, Maple Grove, MN 55369-4924
Phone: 612-425-7653
Fax: 612-493-0310
www.manheim.com

North Star Auto Auction
4908 Valley Industrial Boulevard, North, Shakopee, MN 55379
Phone: 612-445-5544
Fax: 612-445-6773
www.adtauto.com

Saint Cloud Auto Auction
114747 165th Avenue, Becker, MN 55308-8772
Phone: 612-263-8100

MISSISSIPPI
Auto Auction Inc.
Highway 45 North, Baldwyn, MS 38824
Phone: 601-365-2636

Dealers Automobile Auction of the South, Inc.
Highway 51 North, Horn Lake, MS 38637
Phone: 601-393-0500
Fax: 601-393-0599

Dixie Auto Auction
23530 Highway 8 East, Grenada, MS 38901
Phone: 601-226-5637
Fax: 601-227-9060
www.dixmsauc@dixi.net.com

Edge Auto Auction
1308 East Church Street, Booneville, MS 38829-4009
Phone: 601-728-8558

Long Beach Auto Auction
8494 County Farm Road, Long Beach, MS 39560

Phone: 601-452-2030
Fax: 601-452-9588

Mid-South Auto Auction
I-55 North at County Line Road, Ridgeland, MS 39157
Phone: 601-956-2700

Mississippi Auto Auction Inc.
7510 U.S. Highway 49 North, Hattiesburg, MS 39402
Phone: 601-268-7550
Fax: 601-265-3699
www.adtauto.com

Rea Brother's Mid-South Auto Auction
6621 North State Street, Jackson, MS 39213
Phone: 601-956-2700
Fax: 601-956-5603

Thompson Auto Auction Clarksdale
RR-1 # 49A, New Albany, MS 38652-9801
Phone: 601-624-8884

NEBRASKA
Dealers Auto Auction of Nebraska
7500 North 56th Street, Lincoln, NE 68514-9701
Phone: 402-466-8477
Fax: 402-466-7932

Midway Auto Auction Ltd.
115 O Street, Lincoln, NE 68508
Phone: 402-475-5500
Fax: 402-475-5508
members.aol.com/Midwayauct/durst.html

Omaha Auto Auction
9201 South 144th Street, Omaha, NE 68138
Phone: 402-896-8000
Fax: 402-896-6758
www.adtauto.com

Queen City Auto Auction
1104 S. Elm Avenue, Hastings, NE 68901-7142
Phone: 402-463-5294

NEVADA
ISP Auto Auction
9915 North Virginia Street, Reno, NV 89506-9148
Phone: 702-677-2980

Lightning Auctions, Inc.
870 South rock Boulevard, Sparks, NV 89431
Phone: 702-331-4222
Fax: 702-331-4281
www.lightningauctions.com

Manheim's Greater Las Vegas Auto Auction
101 North Mojave Road, Las Vegas, NV 89101
Phone: 702-381-8400
Fax: 702-382-1101
www.manheim.com

Manheim's Greater Nevada Auto Auction
8801 Las Vegas Boulevard South, Las Vegas, NV 89123
Phone: 702-361-1000
Fax: 702-361-5764
www.manheim.com

Nevada Auto Auction
8801 Las Vegas Boulevard South, Las Vegas, NV 89123
Phone: 702-361-1000

Peterson Reno Auto Auction
301 Gentry Way, Reno, NV 89502-4608
Phone: 702-828-2437

TNT Auction
4320 Stephanie Street, Las Vegas, NV 89120
Phone: 702-792-4343

NEW HAMPSHIRE
Auto Auction of New England, Inc.
8 Action Boulevard, Londonderry, NH 03053
Phone: 603-437-5700
Fax: 603-437-5800

NEW JERSEY
ADESA - New Jersey
200 North Main Street, Manville, NJ 08835
Phone: 908-725-2200
Fax: 908-725-2201
www.adesaauctions.com

Country Club Auto Brokers
47 Shrewsbury Avenue, Red Bank, NJ 07701-1129
Phone: 908-741-1129

National Auto Dealers Exchange (N.A.D.E.)
3328 Route 206, Bordentown, NJ 08505
Phone: 609-298-3400

Fax: 609-298-4489
www.manheim.com

Skyline Auto Exchange, Inc.
100 Route 46, Fairfield, NJ 07004
Phone: 973-227-0100
Fax: 973-244-0241
www.adtauto.com/skyline

NEW MEXICO
Albuquerque Auto Auction
3411 Broadway Boulevard, S.E., Albuquerque, NM 87105-0405
Phone: 505-242-9191
Fax: 505-247-7415
www.adtauto.com

NEW YORK
ADESA-Buffalo
12200 Main Street, Akron, NY 14001
Phone: 716-542-3300
Fax: 716-542-3347
www.adesaauctions.com

BQE Public Auction
499 Hamilton Avenue, Brooklyn, NY 11232
Phone: 718-788-5900
Fax: 718-499-0877 www.bqeauction.com

Buffalo Thruway Auto Auction, Inc.
55 Delaware Street, Tonawanda, NY 14150-2217
Phone: 716-743-0055

Central Auto Exchange
20 Cairn Street, Rochester, NY 14611
Phone: 716-328-2277
Fax: 716-328-2311

DCAS Auction
The Brooklyn Navy Yard
Kent Avenue, Brooklyn, NY
Phone: 718-625-1313
Fax: 718-499-0877
www.ci.nyc.us/html/autosche.html

Expressway Auto Auction Inc.
Route 63, South Main Street, Dansville, NY 14437
Phone: 716-335-6071
Fax: 716-335-3486

Newburgh Auto Auction
18 Route 17K, Newburgh, NY 12550
Phone: 914-562-0700
Fax: 914-562-0783
www.manheim.com

N Y Auto Auction
504 Hopkins Street, Buffalo, NY 14220-1417
Phone: 716-822-6420

New York City Police Department
Public Auction of Unclaimed Vehicles
Police Headquarters Auditorium, 1 Police Plaza, Manhattan
www.ci.nyc.us/html/nypd/html/misc/auction.htm

Northway Exchange
Route 146, Clifton Park, NY 12065
Phone: 518-371-7500
Fax: 518-371-0441
www.manheim.com

Rochester-Syracuse Auto Auction, L.P.
Route 414, 1854 Mound Road, Waterloo, NY 13165
Phone: 315-539-5006
Fax: 315-539-9508
www.cag.ca

Stateline Auto Auction, Inc.
830 Tallmadge Hill Road, Waverly, NY 14892
Phone: 607-565-8151
Fax: 607-565-8659 www.state-line-aa.com

Statewide Auto Auction, Inc.
155 Terminal Drive, Plainview, NY 11803-2301
Phone: 516-349-0007

Tri-bore Public Auction
138th Street & the Major Deegan - Exit 3-2500,
Park Avenue Bronx, New York 10451
Phone: 718-AUCTION
Fax: 718-401-4120
www.tri-boro.com

Tri State Auto Auction, Inc.
5930 Route 31, Cicero, NY 13039
Phone: 315-699-2792
Fax: 315-699-9620
www.tristateaa.com

NORTH CAROLINA
ADESA - Charlotte
116000 Fruehauf Drive, Charlotte, NC 28273
Phone: 704-587-7765
Fax: 704-587-9831
www.tristateaa.com

Adcock Auto Auction
1-95 South Bagley Road, Exit 105, Kenly, NC 27542
Phone: 919-284-4052
Fax: 919-284-5706
www.adtauto.com

Ed Radford Auto Auction
8296 U.S. 301 North, Kenly, NC 27542
Phone: 919-284-3004
Fax: 919-284-3005

Greensboro Auto Auction, Inc.
3802 West Wendover Avenue, Greensboro, NC 27407
Phone: 336-299-7777
Fax: 336-854-2689
www.gaauction.com

High Point Auto Auction
6643 Auction Road, High Point, NC 27263
Phone: 336-886-7091
Fax: 336-886-4069
www.manheim.com

Ray's Southern Auto Auction of Greenville
2401 Montreal Avenue, Greensboro, NC 27406

Phone: 910-275-0211
www.raysauction.com

Statesville Auto Auction
I-77 at Exit 54, Statesville, NC 28677
Phone: 704-876-1111
Fax: 704-876-3900
www.manheim.com

NORTH DAKOTA
Tri-State Auto Auction Company, Inc.
1650 East Main Avenue, West Fargo, ND 58078
Phone: 701-282-8203
Fax: 701-281-0888
www.zagroup.com

OHIO
ADESA - Cincinnati/Daytona
4400 William C. Good Boulevard, Franklin, OH 45005
Phone: 513-746-4000
Fax: 513-746-1140
www.adesaauctions.com

ADESA - CLEVELAND
210 East Twinsburg Road, Northfield, OH 44067
Phone: 216-467-8280
Fax: 216-467-2278
www.adesaauction.com

Akron Auto Auction, Inc.
2471 Ley Drive, Akron, OH 44319
Phone: 330-773-8245
Fax: 330-773-1641

Cincinnati Auto Auction
4969 Man Hauser Road, Hamilton, OH 45011
Phone: 513-874-9310
Fax: 513-874-6195
www.sjfgroup.com

Columbus Fair Auto Auction
4700 Groveport Road, Obetz, OH 43207
Phone: 614-497-2000
Fax: 614-497-1132
www.sjfgroup.com

Dayton Auto Auction
7545 North Dixie Drive, Dayton, OH 45414
Phone: 937-454-2292
Fax: 937-454-1056

Gallipolis Auto Auction
286 Upper River Road, Gallipolis, OH 45631
Phone: 614-446-1576
Fax: 614-446-6318

Greater Cleveland Auto Auction
162 Eastland Road, Berea, OH 44017
Phone: 216-234-8108
Fax: 216-234-2709

Montpelier Dealer Auto Auction Inc.
Ohio Turnpike (80/90) Exit 2, Montpelier, OH 43543
Phone: 419-485-3101
Fax: 419-485-5103

Ohio Auto Auction
3905 Jackson Pike, Grove City, OH 43123
Phone: 614-871-2771
Fax: 614-871-6894
www.manheim.com

Toledo Auto Auction Corp.
9797 Fremont Pike, Perrysburg, OH 43551
Phone: 419-872-0872
Fax: 419-872-0748

OKLAHOMA
Altus Auto Auction
Altus, OK 73521
Phone: 405-477-1255

Dealer's Auto Auction of OKC, Inc.
1028 South Portland Avenue, Oklahoma City, OK 73108
Phone: 405-947-2886
Fax: 405-943-8370
Fax: 405-943-6128
www.daaokc.com

El Reno Auto Auction
1930 E. US Highway 66, El Reno, OK 73036-6619
Phone: 405-354-2140

I-44 Auto Auction
16015 East Admiral Place, I-44 East @ 161st Street, Tulsa,
OK 74116
Phone: 918-437-9044
Fax: 918-234-9326

Lewis Poor Boy's Auto Auction
411 Southwest Highway 277, Lawton, OK 73506
Phone: 405-355-8847

Midwest Auto Auction
215 S.E. 61st Street, Oklahoma City, OK 73149
Phone: 405-632-4433
Fax: 405-632-4480
www.mwautoauction.com

Midwest City Auto Auction
5709 South East 15th Street, Oklahoma City, OK 73110-2613
Phone: 405-737-4871

Oklahoma City Auto Auction
5005 South I-35, Oklahoma City, OK 73219
Phone: 405-670-1000
Fax: 405-670-1138

Oklahoma Auto Auctions, Inc.
2932 W. Tecumseh Road, Norman, OK 73069
Phone: 405-364-SOLD (7653)
www.auctionpro.com

Tulsa Auto Auction
8544 East Admiral Place, Tulsa, OK 74115-8139
Phone: 918-832-1050

OREGON
Brusher's Cascade Auto Auction
23585 NE Sandy Boulevard, Wood Village, OR 97060
Phone: 503-492-9200

Fax: 503-492-0115
www.brashers.com

Brusher's Northwest Auto Auction, Inc.
2605 Prairie Road, Eugene, OR 97402
Phone: 541-689-3901
Fax: 541-689-6049
www.brashers.com

Insurance Auto Auctions
4415 N.E. 158th Avenue, Portland, OR 97230
Phone: 503-253-1500
Fax: 503-253-9359
www.home.iaai.com

Insurance Auto Auctions
14335 SW Tualatin-Sherwood Road, Sherwood, OR 97140
Phone: 503-625-5576
Fax: 503-625-6642
www.home.iaai.com

Insurance Auto Auctions
1000 Bethel Drive, Eugene, OR 97402
Phone: 541-689-4000
Fax: 541-689-0083
www.home.iaai.com

Portland Auto Auction
3000 North Hayden Island Drive, Portland, OR 97217
Phone: 503-286-3000
Fax: 503-286-7073
www.manheim.com

Team Venn Gordon Auctioneers
P.O. Box 520, Canby, OR 97013
Phone: 503-266-1551
Fax: 503-263-5700
www.teamvangorden.com

PENNSYLVANIA
ADESA - Pittsburgh
758 Franklin Road, Mercer, PA 16137
Phone: 724-662-4500
Fax: 724-662-2840
www.adesaauctions.com

Aspite Auto Auction
7000 State Road, Philadelphia, PA 19135
Phone: 215-335-4884

Butler Auto Auction
21095 Route 19, Cranberry Township, PA 16066
Phone: 724-452-5555
Fax: 724-452-1310
www.manheim.com

Carriage Trade Auto Auction
1200 Ridge Pike, Conshohocken, PA 19428
Phone: 215-CAR-SALE

Central Pennsylvania Auto Auction, Inc.
Exit 26 of I-80, Lock Haven, PA 17745
Phone: 717-726-4300
Fax: 717-726-7841

Commonwealth Auto Auction
Rural Route 410, Morton, PA 19070
Phone: 610-328-7100
Fax: 610-328-9367
www.quickpage.com/c/commonwealthauto/

Corry Auto Dealers Exchange
12141 Route 6, Corry, PA 16407
Phone: 814-664-7721
Fax: 814-664-7724

D-A Auto Auction
Waltz Mill Road, New Stanton, PA 15672
Phone: 724-722-3122
Fax: 724-722-3087

Danville Auto Dealers Exchange, Inc.
2719 Bloom Road, Danville, PA 17821
Phone: 717-275-2880
Fax: 717-275-5836

Ebensburg Auto Auction, Inc.
3347 New Germany Road, Ebensburg, PA 15931
Phone: 814-472-6019 or 814-471-9969
Fax: 814-472-4273 or 814-472-7735

422 Auto Auction
West Portersville, PA 16051
Phone: 412-368-8885

Garden Spot Auto Auction
Robert Road & Apple Street, Ephrata, PA 17522
Phone: 717-738-7900
Fax: 717-738-7930

Greater Pittsburgh Auto Auction
526 Thompson Run Road, West Mifflin, PA 15122-1321
Phone: 412-464-4340

Harrisburg Auto Auction
1100 South York Street, Mechanicsburg, PA 17055
Phone: 717-697-2222
Fax: 717-697-2234
www.harrisburgaa.com

Hatfield Auto Auction
2280 Bethlehem Pike, Route 309, Hatfield, PA 19440
Phone: 215-822-1935
Fax: 215-822-8140
www.adtauto.com.com

Keystone Auto Auction, Inc.
488 Firehouse Road, Grantville, PA 17028
Phone: 717-469-7900
Fax: 717-469-0311

Manheim Auto Auction
1190 Lancaster Road, Manheim, PA 17545
Phone: 717-665-3571
Fax: 717-665-9265
www.manheim.com

Mason Dixon Auto Auction, Inc.
12876 Molly Pitcher Highway, Greencastle, PA 17225
Phone: 717-597-3121

Pennsylvania Auto Dealers Exchange Inc., (P.A.D.E.)
Interstate 83, Exit 12, York, PA 17405

Phone: 717-266-6611
Fax: 717-266-6522

Perryopolis Auto Auction Inc.
Route 51 South, Perryopolis, PA 15473
Phone: 800-735-5288
Fax: 412-736-0466

Tri-State Auto Auction
55 East Buffalo Church Road, Washington, PA 15301
Phone: 949-225-1777

Willow Street Auto Auction Inc.
Rural Route 2, Willow Street, PA 17584-9802
Phone: 717-464-2761

York Springs Auto Auction
U.S. Route 15, 10 Auction Drive, York Springs, PA 17372
Phone: 800-222-2038
Fax: 717-528-8942
Www, yorkspringsautoauction.com

RHODE ISLAND
Ocean State Auto Auction
Industrial Drive, Exeter, RI 02822
Phone: 401-397-2801
Fax: 401-397-2474

SOUTH CAROLINA
I-85 and Highway 81, Webb Road, Williamston, SC 29697
Phone: 864-231-7000
Fax: 864-231-7900

Clanton's Auto Auction, Inc.
1111 Harry Byrd Highway, Darlington, SC 29532
Phone: 843-393-2861
Fax: 843-395-1521
www.manheim.com

Greenville/Spartanburg Auto Auction
2415 Highway 101 South, Exit 60, I-85, Greer, SC 29651
Phone: 864-801-1199
Fax: 864-801-1084

Hilltop Auto Auction, Inc.
1200 East Buena Vista Avenue, North Augusta, SC 29841
Phone: 800-536-3234
Fax: 803-279-7191

Mayo Auto Auction
4854 Chesnee Highway, Highway 221, Chesnee, SC 29323
Phone: 864-461-9555
Fax: 864-461-3143

Rawls Auto Auction
2818 Pond Branch Road, I-20, Exit 44, Leesville, SC 29070
Phone: 803-657-5111
Fax: 803-657-5910

SOUTH DAKOTA
3715 Beale Street, Rapid City, SD 57703
Phone: 605-342-4971
Fax: 605-341-7861

Sioux Falls Auto Auction
4689-271st Street, Tea, SD 57064
Phone: 800-658-3981
Fax: 605-368-3808 www.serv-net.com

TENNESSEE
ADESA - Knoxville
1011 ADESA Parkway, Lenoir City, TN 37771
Phone: 423-988-8000
Fax: 423-988-5674
www.adesaauctions.com

ADESA - Memphis
5400 Get well Road, Memphis, TN 38118
Phone: 901-365-6300
Fax: 901-365-2795
www.adesaauctions.com

Airport Auto Auction
Airbase Road, Alcoa, TN 37701
Phone: 423-970-9600
Fax: 423-970-9603

Bristol Auto Auction
3298 West State Street, U.S. 11 West @ I-81, Bristol, TN 37621
Phone: 423-764-1148
Fax: 423-764-0279

Chattanooga Auto Auction, LLC
2120 Stein Drive, Chattanooga, TN 37421
Phone: 423-499-0015
Fax: 423-499-0304
www.chatta.com

Clarksville Auto Auction, Inc.
247 Needmore Road, Clarksville, TN 37040
Phone 931-647-5700
Fax: 931-645-3973

East Tennessee Auto Auction
195 Joe McCrary Road, Interstate I-81, Exit 50, Fall Branch, TN 37656
Phone: 423-348-8419
Fax: 423-348-8649

Mid-South Auto Auction
7518 Chapman Highway, Knoxville, TN 37920
Phone: 423-573-7163

Nashville Auto Auction, Inc.
1450 Lebanon Road, Nashville, TN 37210
Phone: 615-244-2140
Fax: 615-255-2047

Tennessee Auto Auction
1815 Old Fort Parkway, Murfreesboro, TN 37129
Phone: 615-890-6292
Fax: 615-896-2933
www.manheim.com

United Auto Auction
3719 Old Get well Road, Memphis, TN 38118
Phone: 90-1-795-5044
Fax: 901-365-8201
www.unitedautorecovery.com

TEXAS

ADESA - Austin
2108 Ferguson Lane, Austin, TX 78754
Phone: 512-873-4000
Fax: 512-873-4022
www.adesaauctions.com

ADESA - Dallas
1224-E Big Town Boulevard, Mesquite, TX 75149
Phone: 972-288-7585
www.adesaauctions.com

ADESA - Houston
4526 North Sam Houston Parkway, Houston, TX 77066
Phone: 713-692-3322
www.jturpin@adesa.com

ADESA - San Antonio
200 South Callaghan Road, San Antonio, TX 78227
Phone: 210-434-4999
Fax: 210-431-0645
www.adesaauctions.com

Amarillo Auto Auction Inc.
7801 IH 40 East, Amarillo, TX 79104
Phone: 806-345-5600

Big H Auto Auction
14450 West Road, Houston, TX 77041
Phone: 281-890-4300
Fax: 281-890-7953
www.manheim.com

Big State Auto Auction
6657 Highway 80 West, Abilene, TX 79605
Phone: 915-698-4391
Fax: 915-691-0263

Callaway's Cleburne Auto Auction
3825 North Main, Cleburne, TX 76031
Phone: 817-643-0003
Fax: 817-558-2101

Cedar Creek Auto Auction
Highway 175W, Mabank, TX 75147
Phone: 903-887-7116

Dallas Auto Auction, Inc.
5333 West Kiest Boulevard, Dallas, TX 75236-1055
Phone: 214-330-1800
Fax: 214-339-9361 www.adtauto.com

Dealers Auto Auction of Dallas
2717 East Main, Grand Prairie, TX 75050
Phone: 972-339-4100
Fax: 972-264-2086
www.manheim.com

Dealers Auto Auction of El Paso
485 Coates Drive & I-10, West El Paso, TX 79932
Phone: 915-833-9333

East Texas Auto Auction
2910 West Erwin Street, Tyler, TX 75701-6623
Phone: 903-593-7347

First Choice Auto Auction
825 Rankin Road, Houston, TX 77073
Phone: 281-821-2300
Fax: 281-821-2977

Fort Worth Auto Auction
2245 Jacksboro Highway, Fort Worth, TX 76114
Phone: 817-626-5494
Fax: 800-544-9414
www.manheim.com

Gaston & Sheehan
1420 Highway 685, P.O. Box 856, Pflugerville, TX 78691
Phone: 512-251-2780
Fax: 512-990-2900
www.austin.citysearch.com

Houston Auto Auction
3040 Woodridge, Houston, TX 77087
Phone: 713-644-1085 www.houston-auctions.com

Houston Insurance Auto Auctions
12575 Hiram Clarke Road, Houston, TX 77045
Phone: 713-721-5611
Fax: 713-721-7530

Corpus Christi Insurance Auto Auctions
4701 Agnes Street, Corpus Christi, TX 78405
Phone: 512-881-9555
Fax: 512-887-8880

Grand Prairie Insurance Auto Auctions
4226 E. Main Street, Grand Prairie, TX 75050

Phone: 872-642-4445
Fax: 972-642-6283

Humble Insurance Auto Auctions
6875 Will Clayton Parkway, Humble, TX 77338
Phone: 281-540-6655
Fax: 281-540-9040

San Antonio Insurance Auto Auctions
10475 Somerset Road, San Antonio, TX 78211
Phone: 210-623-1111
Fax: 210-623-1227

Lakeside Auto Auction, L.C.
1810 East Interstate 30, Rockwall, TX 75087
Phone: 972-771-9919
Fax: 972-722-4827

Fort Worth and State Wide Lone Star Auctioneers
2315 North Main, Suite 300, Fort Worth, TX 76106-8573
Phone: 817-740-9400 or 817-429-3336
Fax: 817-740-9777

Lone Star Auto Auction of Lubbock
2706 Slaton Highway, Lubbock, TX 79404
Phone: 806-745-6606
Fax: 806-745-9280

Lubbock Auto Auction, Inc.
1122 East 34th Street, Lubbock, TX 79404
Phone: 806-744-1444
Fax: 806-763-1214

Manheim's Dealers Auto Auction of El Paso
485 Coates, El Paso, TX 79932
Phone: 915-833-9333
Fax: 915-833-9390
www.manheim.com

Midland Odessa Auto Auction
2521 North Macro Avenue, Odessa, TX 79761
Phone: 915-376-3063
Fax: 915-367-3358

Montgomery County Auto Auction
Highway 105 East, Conroe, TX 77301
Phone: 409-788-2881

Pasadena Auto Auction
9605 Old Galveston Road, Houston, TX 77034
Phone: 713-948-0001
Fax: 713-948-0300

Public Auto Auction Company
3200 East Randolph Mill Road, Arlington, TX 76011-6838
Phone: 817-640-6227

San Antonio Auto Auction
2042 Ackerman Road, San Antonio, TX 78219
Phone: 210-661-4200
Fax: 800-621-1705
www.manheim.com

South Texas Auto Auction
501 East Nolana, Pharr, TX 78577

Phone: 956-781-1431
Fax: 956-781-1202

Sparkling City Auto Auction of Corpus Christi
3200 Anges, Corpus Christi, TX 78469
Phone: 512-887-7653
Fax: 512-887-6559

Texarkana Auto Auction
903 Elm Street, Texarkana, TX 75501-5015
Phone: 903-794-6925

Texas Auto Traders Auctioneers
841- North Highway, Houston, TX 7703702808
Phone: 713-862-5900

United Liquidators Public Auto Auction
3404 Ft. Worth Highway, Weatherford, TX 76087
Phone: 817-613-9191
Fax: 817-613-9830

U.S.A. Auto Auction, Inc.
3208 East 10th, Amarillo, TX 79104
Phone: 806-374-8982
Fax: 806-374-8984

Waco Auto Auction
5100 South Loop #340, Waco, TX 76706-4636
Phone: 817-662-3855

UTAH

Brashner's Salt Lake Auto Auction
780 South 5600 West, Salt lake City, UT 84104
Phone: 801-322-1234
Fax: 801-322-1315
www.brashers.com

TNT Auction
2353 N. Redwood Road, Salt Lake City, UT 84116
Phone: 801-519-0123
Fax: 801-519-0124

Utah Auto Auction
1650 West 500 South, Woods Cross, UT 84087-2226
Phone: 801-298-7900
Fax: 801-298-9209
www.manheim.com

Utah Auto Sales
10 North State, Lindon, UT 84003
Phone: 801-796-7700

VIRGINIA

Atlantic Auctions Limited
1195 Lance Road, Norfolk, VA 23502
Phone: 757-461-1501 Fax: 757-461-1239

Atlantic Auto Auctions, Ltd.
641 West Southside Plaza Street, Richmond, VA 23224-1721
Phone: 804-232-1580

Buchanan Auto & Auction, Inc., II
3856 South Military Highway, Chesapeake, VA 23323

Phone: 757-487-2175 or 757-485-3342
Fax: 757-487-1213
www.buchananauction.com

Dominion Auto Auction Inc.
15246 Lee Highway, Bristol, VA 24202-4010
Phone: 703-669-6816

Fredericksburg Auto Auction
4907 Jefferson Davis Highway, Fredericksburg, VA 22408
Phone: 540-898-4900
Fax: 540-898-3759
www.manheim.com

Harrisonburg Auto Auction
3560 Early Road, Harrisonburg, VA 22801
Phone: 540-434-5991
Fax: 540-434-6813
www.manheim.com

Leesburg Public Auto Auction
18 Fort Evans Road, Leesburg, VA 20176
Phone: 703-777-7777
Fax: 703-777-7043 or 757-461-1239

Radford Auto Auction, Inc.
2500 Tyler Road, Radford, VA 24141
Phone: 540-639-9011
Fax: 540-639-0744
www.radfordautoauction.com

Tidewater Auto Auction
3316 South Military Highway, Chesapeake, VA 23323
Phone: 757-487-3464
Fax: 757-485-2227
www.tidewaterautoauction.com

Tysons Public Auto Auction
8610 Leesburg Pike, Tysons Corner, VA 22182
Phone: 703-442-0100
www.tysonsautoauction.com

WASHINGTON
Bellingham Public Auto Auction
1251 Verona Street, Bellingham, WA 98226-2220
Phone: 360-647-5370

Dealers Auto Auction of Spokane
2215 South Hanford Road, Spokane, WA 99224
Phone: 509-244-4500
Fax: 509-244-8244

Elis Auction, Inc.
2042 - 112th Street, South Tacoma, WA 98404
Phone: 1-800-244-1946

Auburn Insurance Auto Auctions
3130 D Street South East, Auburn, WA 98002
Phone: 253-735-2724
Fax: 253-735-3945

Spokane Insurance Auto Auctions
2221 South Garfield Road, Spokane, WA 99224

Phone: 509-244-3464
Fax: 509-244-9672

Seattle: James G. Murphy Company
18226 68th Avenue North East, Bothell, WA 98011
Phone: 206-486-1246
Fax: 206-483-8247

Olympus Public Auto Auction
1845 93rd Avenue Southwest, Olympus, WA 98512
Phone: 360-352-2646

Stokes Auction, Inc.
8398 Spring Creek Road SE, Port Orchard, WA 98367
Phone: 360-876-0236

Puget Sound Auto Auction, Inc.
621 - 37th Street, N.W. Auburn, WA 98002
Phone: 253-735-1600
Fax: 253-351-0320
www.adtauto.com

South Seattle Auto Auction
19443 - 77th Ave. South, Kent, WA 98032
Phone: 206-762-1600
Fax: 253-395-3342
www.manheim.com

Woodinville Public Auto Auction
13820 North East 195th, Woodinville, WA 98072-1664
Phone: 800-243-2227

WEST VIRGINIA
Capital City Auto Auction
5100 Elk River Road North, Elkview, WV 25071
Phone: 304-965-2277
Fax: 304-965-2284

Moore's Auction Service
RR 2, Fairview, WV 26570-9802
Phone: 304-798-3141

Morgantown Auto Auction
Box 1228, Morgantown, WV 26505
Phone: 304-328-5851
Fax: 304-328-5854

Mountain State Auto Auction
Interstate I-79, Exit 125, Shinnston, WV 26431
Phone: 304-592-5300
Fax: 304-592-3510

WISCONSIN
ADESA - Wisconsin
W10415 State Road 33, Portage, WI 53901
Phone: 608-742-8245
Fax: 608-742-4415
www.adesaauctions.com

Central Wisconsin Auto Auctions, Inc.
9107 Schofield Avenue, Schofield, WI 54476
Phone: 715-359-8495
Fax: 715-359-7895

Fox Valley Auto Auction
3266 Williams Grant Drive, De Pere, WI 54115-5275
Phone: 920-336-3121
Fax: 920-532-4588

PUERTO RICO
Manheim's Caribbean Auto Dealers Exchange
Canovanas Puerto Rico
Phone: 787-256-5666

CANADA
Manheim's Oshawa Dealers Exchange
Phone: 800-263-1962

Manheim's Toronto Auto Auction
Milton Ontario
Phone: 905-275-3000

UNITED KINGDOM
Manheim UK • Leeds
Phone: 01144-113-282-8686

FRANCE
Manheim France • Bordeaux
Phone: 01133-557-924-700

AUSTRALIA
Manheim's Fowles Auction Group
Phone: 01161-392-545-555

Internet
Sources

Making Money
From Online Sources.

100 Plus Sources

From Your Home Computer.

Finding Your Niche.

Internet Sources

Making money from on line sources. This volume is a list that we compiled of Internet Sources of Information. There are literally thousands of sites to gather information about buying and selling cars. Some sites cater to the public to list their cars for sale and others are more geared towards the Dealer information to buy and sell.

We have tried to list the more popular sites that we feel would be more beneficial in your new venture. Please look through our list, make notes by the ones that you feel would be more beneficial to you. Some sell parts, some sell cars, some sell services, you can always find the information you need, if you look deep enough.

As in any manuals, we can only direct you to the site. You will have to put some effort out on researching for any additional information that will help you succeed in the car business.

The Internet is a world of information, take full advantage of this free information.

ON-LINE SOURCES

- Buy cars like dealers do
  http://www.ACAusction.com
  San Francisco East Bay Area

  _____

  _____

  _____

- 5000+ Auction Events
  http://www.bargain.com
  Repossessed and seized property

  _____

  _____

  _____

- PoliceAuctions.com
  http://www.policeauctions.com
  Cars from $500, seized, unclaimed, etc.

  _____

  _____

  _____

- Bargain Network Cars
  http://www.bargain.com
  Find Bargains on autos, homes, etc. Live auctions too.

  _____

  _____

  _____

- Online Auctions. Auto auction, not, eBay
  http://www.greatvehicles.com/pops3.html
  Online Vehicle Auction

  _____

  _____

  _____

- Police Auctions; Government Auctions Locally
  http://www.autobeyond.com/Information.htm

  _____

  _____

  _____

- IBM Customer success stories for customer Copart Salvage Auto
  **http://www-3.ibm.com/software/success/cssdb.nsf/
  bycustomerVW?**

  _____

  _____

  _____

- Palm handhelds got to work at auto auctions
  **http://www.palmpowerenterprise.com/issue/
  issue200111/auction001.html**

  _____

  _____

  _____

- FirstGov - Shopping and Auction - Cars & Transportation
  http://www.firstgov.gov/shopping/cars/cars.shtml
  Customs Seized Vehicle Auctions

  _____

  _____

  _____

- Auctions Expert International - Internet Sales & Marketing
  http://www.auctionsexpert.com

  _____

  _____

  _____

- Top 10 Car Dealer Scams
  http://www.carbuyingtips.com
  New car buying guide, haggle tips, used car buying tips

  _____

  _____

  _____

- Government Auctions
  http://www.streetupdate.com/auction/
  Cheap cars & Trucks

  _____

  _____

  _____

- Auctions
  http://www.Shopping.com

  _____

  _____

  _____

- Government Auctions Guide
  http://www.government-auctions-guide.com
  1500+ Live & Online Gov't Auctions

  _____

  _____

  _____

- Online Auctions
  http://www.online----auctions.com/

  _____

  _____

  _____

- New Jersey State Auto Auction
  http://www.njstateauto.com

  _____

  _____

  _____

• Open Directory - Shopping: Auctions: Autos
http://dmoz.org/Shopping/Auctions/Autos
Copart Auto International

_____

_____

_____

The Ultimate Guise - Classifieds2000.com
http://www.classifieds2000.com
New and Used

_____

_____

_____

• Manheim Auto Auctions Inc.
http://www.ftc.gov/opa/2000/10/manhheim.htm

_____

_____

_____

• Copart Salvage Auto Auctions Inquiries and Feedback
http://www.copart/com/feedback

_____

_____

_____

• Access Auto Auction - Auto Government Car Auctions
http://www.accessautoauction.com

_____

_____

_____

• Free Online Auto Information on New Used Cars
http://www.carjunky.com
Free Internet Automotive Directory

_____

_____

_____

• Auctions: Government Auto Car Auctions
http://www.allautoauctions.com

_____

_____

_____

• NASA Auto Auctions
http://www.eizo.com/profile/nasa/contents.html

_____

_____

_____

• RM Classic Cars
http://www.rmcars.com

_____

_____

_____

• Federal Government Auto Auctions, US and Canada
http://www.fedautoauction.com

_____

_____

_____

• Barrett-Jackson Auction Company
http://www.barrett-jackson.com

• Invoice Dealers.com
http://www.InvoiceDealers.com

• On-line Auction Sites
http://www.on-line-auction-sites.com

• AutoGuide.net: The Internet's Largest Automotive Directory
http://www.autoguide.net/buyandsell/auction.shtml

• Auto Auctions
http://www.motorzoo.com/Automotive.AutoAuctions. htmls· investing in America: Auto Auctions
http://money.know-more.com/MONEY.asp?IOID=960

• LAB Auto Auctions
http://www.lab-auction.com/home.htm

_____

_____

_____

• LLDC.Com - Auto Auctions - Chat
http://www.lldc.com/chat

_____

_____

_____

• Yahoo! Autos - Buy a Car
http://autos.yahoo.com/buy.html?refsrc=autos/credit
The Pricing Maze - How to get the best deal

_____

_____

_____

• Manheim Auctions
http://www.manheimauctions.com

_____

_____

_____

• Toronto Bookmarks
http://www.samarins.com/toronto/links.html

_____

_____

_____

- BSC America
  http://www.bscamerica.com
  - LLDC Luxury Car Auctions
  http://www.lldc.com

_____

_____

_____

- Auto Forum
  http://www.autoforum.sk
  Useful Information about Cars

_____

_____

_____

- FedWin government auto auctions
  http://www.fedwin.com/site_map.asp

_____

_____

_____

- Automoti.com
  http://www.automoti.com
  Find used cars and auto auction from all USA

_____

_____

_____

- CarsforSale.com
  http://www.carsforsale.com

- Automotive News
  http://www.autonews.com/page.cms?pageId=85

- Google Directory - Shopping> Auctions> Autos
  http://directory.google.com/Top/Shopping/Auctions/Autos/

- GSA Fleet Vehicle Sales
  http://www.autoauctions.gsa.gov· Insurance Auto Auctions
  http://www.iaai.com

- Auto Salvage Sale
  http://www.salvageauto.com

• ADESA Online
http://www.adesa.com

_____

_____

_____

• Kruse International
http://www.kruseinternational.com

_____

_____

_____

• Brusher's Auto Auction
http://www.brashers.com

_____

_____

_____

• RanchMart.com
http://www.Ranchmart.com
Free ads to sell vehicles

_____

_____

_____

• CarsDirect.com
http://www.carsdirect.com

_____

_____

_____

- Autoweb.com
  http://www.autoweb.com

  _____

  _____

  _____

- Auto Trader
  http://www.autotrader.com

  _____

  _____

  _____

- The Orange County Registers' Car Finder
  http://www.occarfinder.com

  _____

  _____

  _____

- EBay - The World's Largest Online Marketplace
  http://www.ebay.com

  _____

  _____

  _____

- Kelly Blue Book
  http://www.kbb.com

  _____

  _____

  _____

- Squiz-Motors - free UK Car Auction
  http:www.squiz-motors.co.uk

  _____

  _____

  _____

- Police Seized Cars $100
  http://www.dealerznet.com

  _____

  _____

  _____

- Auction Sniper
  http://www.auctionsniper.com

  _____

  _____

  _____

- uBid.com
  http://www.uBid.com

  _____

  _____

  _____

- Robertson Auto Auctions
  http://www.robertsonleasing.com

  _____

  _____

  _____

- US Government Auto Auctions
http://www.autoauctions.gsa.gov/whatandhow.cfm

_____

_____

_____

- Auto Group
http://www.auto-group.com.au/home/default.asp

_____

_____

_____

- Classic-CarAuction.com
http://www.classic-carauction.com

_____

_____

_____

- Auto Government Auctions

- Price Quotes
http://www.pricequotes.com
Compare Care Dealers

_____

_____

_____

- Motorzoo.com
http://www.motorzoo.com

_____

_____

_____

- Autobytel
  http://www.autobytel.com

  _____

  _____

  _____

- Zeemo
  http://www.zeemo.com
  Free online selling

  _____

  _____

  _____

- Moto seller
  http://www.motoseller.com
  Used vehicles for sale by owner

  _____

  _____

  _____

- Bayoubid
  http://www.bayoubid.com

  _____

  _____

  _____

- Used Car Mart
  http://www.usedcarmart.co.uk

  _____

  _____

  _____

- 2buycars.net
  http://www.2buycars.net

  _____

  _____

  _____

- Trader Online Classified Ads
  http://www.traderonline.com

  _____

  _____

  _____

- Classics Cars.com
  http://www.classicscars.com
  Ferrari, Lamborghini, Maserati, Pagani Zonda, Alfa, Porsche, etc.

  _____

  _____

  _____

- Cars for Sale Locally
  http://www.carsdirect.com
  Choose from a complete selection. Instant pricing with no obligation

  _____

  _____

  _____

- Cars for Sale
  http://www.autoweb.com
  Complete Auto Research View Prices Specs & Photos here!

  _____

  _____

  _____

- Auto Classifieds
  http://www.autos.nytimes.com
  Buy or sell your car. Detailed listings expert reviews and more!

  _____

  _____

  _____

- Carsmart.com
  http://www.carsmart.com

  _____

  _____

  _____

- Repossessed Car Auctions
  http://www.aCheapCarFindercom
  Get access top nationwide seized cars auction database. All Makes!

  _____

  _____

  _____

- Livedeal.com
  http://www.livedeal.com
  Local buyers & sellers - Online Avoid the hassle & cost of shipping

  _____
  _____
  _____

- State Police Auctions
  http://www.policeauctions.com
  Cars from $500

  _____
  _____
  _____

- Netcom3.com
  http://www.netcom3.com

  _____
  _____
  _____

- Auto Trade Zone
  http://www.autotradezone.com

  _____
  _____
  _____

- MotoSeller
  http://www.motoseller.com

  _____

  _____

  _____

- Cars America
  http://www.carsamerica.com

  _____

  _____

  _____

- AutoWorm.com
  http://www.autoworm.com

  _____

  _____

  _____

- Car Buying Tips
  http://www.carbuyingtips.com

  _____

  _____

  _____

- My Car Network
  http://www.45609.mycarnetwork.com

  _____

  _____

  _____

- Price Quites
  http://www.pricequotes.com

  _____

  _____

  _____

- Buying Advice
  http://www.buyingadvice.com

  _____

  _____

  _____

- Edmunds
  http://www.edmunds.com

  _____

  _____

  _____

- Why Pay Sticker.com
  http://www.whypaysticker.com

  _____

  _____

  _____

- The Toyota Lineup
  http://www.toyota.com/dealer

  _____

  _____

  _____

- AutoGuide.net: The Internet's Largest Automotive Directory
  http://www.autoguide.net/buyandsell/auction.shtml

  _____

  _____

  _____

- Carfax Reports
  http://www.carfax.com

  _____

  _____

  _____

- Automotive World Analysis
  http://www.automotiveworld.com

  _____

  _____

  _____

- Auto Industry Research
  http://www.autoresearcher.com

  _____

  _____

  _____

- Auto Industry Reports
  http://www.harrisinfo.com

  _____

  _____

  _____

- Industrial Forecasts
  http://www.industrialinfo.com

  _____

  _____

  _____

- Automotive Industry
  http://www.us.go4.it
  All things automotive Massive directory of information

  _____

  _____

  _____

- Automotive Mkt Research
  http://www.internationalbusinessstrategies.com

  _____

  _____

  _____

  - FREE CAR INSPECTION CHECK LIST
  - www.AutoCheck101.com

Locating
Service

NO-RISK-HUGE PROFITS
"WORKING SMART"

LOCATING SERVICE / AUTO BROKER .....

Another Avenue for additional Car Profits

If you are not completely sold on the idea of taking the risk of buying and selling cars with your own money or you want to get into the business in a more subtle way, you may want to consider staring a locating service for customers who are interested in getting a particular car. A locating service / Auto Broker, can be thought of as being a personal shopper or buyer for your customers. It is important that you follow all the steps outlined in Chapters 1 through 3, as they will give you a basic understanding of what you should be looking for when you go to find the desired vehicles. Many individuals make a living off of simply locating cars for customers or dealerships.

Throughout over twenty years of experience in the automobile industry, operating a locating service for vehicle is one of my favorite ways to make Car Profits. This is a low pressure opportunity with little to no risk. You can set you fees however you want, but most customers and professionals charge about six percent of the purchase price. Just think, if you located and sold ten cars at an average purchase price of $15,000 you would make $9,000. The best part about a locating service is that the car is sold to your customer before you ever buy it from the auction!

Getting Started

Promoting your services to potential buyer is probably the most important thing you can do in this arena. Word will spread very fast that you are able to perform this service once you have successfully located cars for people. It is not uncommon for satisfied customers to send two or three friends my way after they see what a quality vehicle they purchased at a discounted price. A good place to start is with your friends, family and co-workers who may be interested in purchasing a car. Now that people around me know that I have the ability to save them money and get them the exact car they want, they constantly want to know when we can help them purchase their new car. Of course, advertising in the classifieds, sending direct mail pieces or leaving literature at heavy traffic areas will also help to quickly spread the existence of your new car Locating Service. A typical advertisement could go like this:

EXAMPLE AD:

TIRED OF PAYING RETAIL FOR A CAR?
John's Vehicle Locating Service
We will find the exact make and model you want to buy at
Wholesale prices
well below retail value. We specialize in locating exotic foreign
cars and quality sport utility vehicles.
Call 212-555-1212 for more information

Once you have established yourself as a dependable and trustworthy avenue for locating vehicles, it should not shock you to search for ten to twenty cars for customers at one time. On very attractive aspect of locating vehicle for people is that they will save money when buying a vehicle. This method of purchasing a vehicle will generally save your customers significant money when compared to buying a car form the traditional car lot. As a rule of thumb, we would estimate that customers can save between $2,000 and $5,000 depending on the type of vehicle they purchase.

This method of making Car Profits is very service oriented and sometimes requires you to spend additional one on one time with your customers. It is very important to know exactly what they are searching for because at some point you will be selecting the car that they will be purchasing.

This manual includes a sample Locating Agreement that you can use and modify to create your very own form. At the outset of starting your Locating Service, you can put this form into your computer or take it to a print shop and make the necessary modifications. Then when you have your first customer you can take the time to tell them about your service and go through this form with them step by step.

Educate Your Customer
When you find a potential customer who wants you to locate a vehicle for them, you will need to educate them about the process, pricing and your fee. Explaining the process is crucial to ensure that there are no surprises down the road. In this business you should tell your customer that you will help them narrow down the type of vehicle that they want, and then you will search for a vehicle that meets their description. Once you locate the vehicle, usually at an auction, you will contact them and describe the vehicle to them. Upon their approval, proceed to bid on the vehicle staying under your customers "top price" for the vehicle. If you buy the car for them, then you will bring it home and complete the transaction.

The most important thing that you will need to find out is EXACTLY what they want to buy. Let us say someone comes to you and says they want a foreign four-door sedan. That is simply not enough. Encourage them to go look at vehicles that meet that general description and decide on one or two specific models. Make sure that they specify the features that they must have, would like and will live with. Allowing some flexibility is OK, but do not let their description vary too much or you may come home with something they do not like.

Set Your Fee / Contract
Now that you have helped your customer decide what type of vehicle they want you to buy for them and educated them about the process, you should have them read and sign the Locating Agreement. It is crucial that they fill out the second page of the Locating Agreement, which sets forth the vehicle choices and features that they want on their new car. This Locating Agreement is a contract between you and the customer and it will be written evidence of what they have requested for you to buy them. Remember, when filling this out, the more detail the better. This will save you headaches down the road if a customer wants to change their mind after the car is purchased.

As a part of the contract you will need to make sure that your customers give you a rock solid "top of the line" purchase price. This amount will be your key to know exactly how much they are willing to pay for the car. Of course, this figure may not include you fees, taxes and other minor expenses, but you will save yourself many problems if you force your customers to commit to a ceiling price on their vehicle.

While setting the contract up, you should decide on how you will charge your customer and explain it to them in detail. As we stated earlier, most professionals in this business will charge a flat percentage fee on the value of the car purchased. To ensure that you always make some money for the work of locating the car, it is recommended that you also have a base fee. For example, you could tell a customer that you will buy any car they want for 6% of the purchase price or $700 fee whichever is greater.

Some dealers operate under the premise that they will buy customers a certain car chosen and the customer will pay the agreed upon price, regardless of how much the dealer actually paid for the car. Even if they buy it for thousands of dollars less than the agreed upon price, they still charge that amount and in essence inflate their profits. While this is an acceptable way of doing business, experience has proven that a minimum amount and percentage of purchase price helps to keep you and the customer happy. It is very difficult to explain to a customer that you paid $4,000 for this car and you charged them $7,000. Using the percentage method of charging you customers also avoids the minor problems that your customers may find with the car, such as scratches, interior wear, etc. If they feel like they were taken, customers can make your life very unpleasant. That is why we recommend the percentage basis.

It is very important to assure your customer that you will work with them to find the best vehicle to meet their desires. Assure them that if you do not find the vehicle they want in four weeks, you will return their deposit. Getting to the point of returning a deposit rarely happens, but when you make it a point to show this to your customers, they will feel very at ease and comfortable with you and your locating service.

Buying the Vehicle

Once the contract is signed and you have been charged with locating a vehicle for your customer, the fun begins. Searching the auctions for the right car can be challenging, however once you have a bit of experience you will find that it is not as difficult as first thought. A few things you may want to do to make the search easier is to check your auctions internet website and see when your customers desired vehicle will be coming up. It is always helpful to show up to the auction lot either the day before the auction or very early the morning of the sale. This will give you plenty of time to scour the lot and find the vehicle your customer wants. It is strongly recommended that once you find a vehicle or two that would interest your customer, you take the time to call them and tell them about the vehicle. Walk around the car and describe it to them over the phone. Be honest with them…..tell them about the condition is a very truthful manner and don't try to hide problems such as scratches, interior wear, air conditioning problems, etc. They are going to see the car very soon if you buy it and that is not the time for them to find out about obvious problems.

Give them an honest assessment of the car over the telephone and then find out if they want you to bid on the car. Once you get the verbal approval and you are aware of their "top of the line" price, you should go and bid on the car when it comes to the auction block.

If you buy the vehicle it is always helpful and re-assuring to have the auction mechanic look over the car to make sure that there are no fatal flaws associated with the vehicle. The things they will normally look for are frame damage, water damage and other obvious problems. For peace of mind for you and your customer, it is a good idea to have this check done if there are any doubts. This service could be an additional charge, but it is well worth it to assure your customer that they have bought a reputable vehicle.

The great thing about a Locating Service is that once you have satisfied one customer via telephone, you can go right back to work on other customers who have hired you to locate vehicle for them. It is not uncommon to find and purchase three to five vehicles for separate customers in one day at the auction. This is where the real money is made!

Finalizing the Transaction

Providing the purchaser with an itemized list of figures involved in the transaction is always helpful and helps to show them that you are operating a respectable operation. There are different schools of thought on whether or not you want to show the customer the actual price you paid for the vehicle at the auction. We have always operated under the theory that if you agree on your payment or percentage before you buy their car, then showing the customer the actual price actually helps your business. The customer is assured that they are not being taken advantage of. Because there are other costs associated with the purchase of the vehicle, we recommend that you give the customer a breakdown of costs along with the final paperwork for purchase. A typical breakdown for the purchase of a vehicle should look something like this:

Vehicle Cost	$15,000.
Auction Cost	$ 350.
Floor plan Fee	$ 85.
Interest Cost (4 days @ ___%)	$ 75.
Tax ($15,000 x 6%)	$ 622.
Tag Transfer Fee	$ 110.
Locating Service Fee	
(6% of $10,000 or $700 Min	**$ 900.**
(Your Profit)	
TOTAL CUSTOMER COST	***$17,142.***

As you can see the Car Profit for you is very respectable and your customer has received a great deal on the purchase of their new vehicle. When delivering the car to your customer, one thing that always helps is to spend the extra few bucks and get the car washed and cleaned out before you present it to the buyer. You are buying a used car and there will always be something that does not look brand new, however the first time your client sees the car will they will form an opinion on how you did for them. Word of mouth is the best form of advertising and making your customers happy will ensure that they will spread the word about your car Locating Service.

In these days of mega car dealerships and hungry car salesmen, you customers will find this locating service to be a breath of fresh air. They will have the opportunity to work with a professional like you and save money. The whole time they will find the car that they desire and avoid the hassle of traditional car buying. The best thing for you is that you will have the opportunity to make huge Car Profits by locating vehicles in a low risk, low pressure environment!

Have a Company Policy and Standards:

In operating a locating service or any business, I have found that you must always remember your ABC's – Attitude, Belief and Character. Maintain a good attitude; this will take you a long way in life. You attitude will determine your altitude! Believe in yourself. You have the power to do whatever you want, but you must first believe you can do it before any dream becomes a reality. Always act with integrity and good Character. Your business will prosper and succeed once you establish the reputation that you operate with Character. I would recommend a business plan also, can be purchased at www.CarBusiness101.com

EXAMPLE BELOW: Is a format of a Locating Agreement, Please adjust / edit to fit your needs and requirements.

Office: 407-555-5555
Fax::   407-555-5555
Cell: 407-555-5555
Email:

You're Company
123 Main St.
Your Town, USA 12345

Locating Vehicle Sales Agreement

Dear Customer:

(YOUR COMPANY) will find and purchase a vehicle solely for you, (the purchaser) as close as possible to your match as described below. Keep in mind, used vehicles are all different in conditions and equipment, you are not ordering a new vehicle from the factory to be built to your specifications. I will attempt to find the closest match, with condition and value in your best interest.

Purchaser agrees to compensate (YOUR COMPANY) with a 6% fee of the purchaser price of the vehicle, with $700.00 as a minimum fee. A 10% Deposit of the estimated amount of the vehicle to be purchased with is required to start the locating service. If vehicle is not found within 4 weeks of this agreement, if requested by purchaser the deposit will be refunded and agreement terminated.

(YOUR COMPANY) will pay for the vehicle the day of the sale, with check or Floor Plan money, if the customer does not pay the balance the day of purchase, company will use Floor Plan money (credit line) to pay for the vehicle, and purchase agrees to pay for any fees and interest resulting in this purchase. In addition, purchaser should have his/her monies arranged for balance, due within 3 business days unless other arrangements are made prior, and noted below.

If for any reason purchaser cannot pay balance due within agreed time, (YOUR COMPANY) will resell purchased said purchased vehicle at the auction, and purchaser agrees to pay (YOUR COMPANY) the agreed buyer's fee, plus an additional $500.00 selling fee for extra time and handling. These fees along with auction fees and transportation costs will be taken out of the deposit, and any surplus difference will be refunded, if deposit is short of covering expenses & fees, customer agrees to pay balance upon receipt. If not paid within 2 days if receipt, customer agrees to pay for any collection fees that may occur.

Both parties agree that this is a legal and enforceable agreement, between purchaser and (YOUR COMPANY).

Page 1 of 3   Initial _____

• Page 2

	1st Choice:	2nd Choice:	3rd Choice
Year:			
Make			
Model:			
Doors.			
Ext./Color:			
Int. Color			
Leather:			
Cloth:			
Sunroof:			
Power:			
Windows:			
Seats:			
C-D:			
Miles:			
A.Must:			
Price Range:			
Remarks:			

Page 2 of 3   Initial _____

Page 3

Continuation of Locating / Sales Agreement

Purchaser:_____   _____
                    Print   Signature

Co-Purchaser:

_____   _____
          Print   Signature

Address:_____   _____

City: _____ State: _____ Zip: _____

Phone # _____ Date: _____

(YOUR COMPANY)

_____   _____
          Print   Signature

Date _____   DepositCollected$_____

Dear Entrepreneur:

I want to thank you for purchasing my book. Myself and a few dealer friends have put many hours into it, so it may be the best value and information possible. I want you to have every opportunity to get off on the right foot in your new venture. I have over twenty years in the car business, and have seen many dealers make a ton of money! My goal is to give you the best insight and guidance so you may be the most successful in your town.

If you are serious about getting into this exciting business of cars, you should be able to be up and running in a matter of 4 to 5 weeks. First you will need to ask yourself, if this is what you really want to do. Life is too short not to be happy in your work. I have to tell you, it has been exciting for me for over 20 years.

I have set up a web site: www.CarBusiness101.com / www. AutoCheck101.com for a FREE Inspection Check List to Print out. My intention is to continually be adding important links and other information about getting into the car business. Please keep checking back as it will be a work in progress.

I wish you the best of luck in your new venture, if you bought on Amazon.com and you feel that this book may help you with your new venture, Please leave me a good review, so I can help other's achieve their dreams.

I know there are people reading this book, and some may like it an other's may not, but remember, everyone is at a different level, I am trying to cover the beginner also.

Want to Thank You in advance for trusting in me with this small purchase, and I really hope that you find your dream too !

John DaRe

www.CarBusiness101.com
www.AutoCheck101.com Get your Free Inspection Check list !

Made in the USA
Lexington, KY
28 June 2014